KENNETH C.

ILLUSTRATED BY TOM BLOOM

DON'T KNOW MUCH ABOUT®

PLANET EARTH

HarperCollins*Publishers*

ACKNOWLEDGMENTS

An author's name goes on the cover of a book. But behind that book are a great many people who make it all happen. I would like to thank all of the wonderful people at HarperCollins who helped make this book a reality, including Susan Katz, Kate Morgan Jackson, Barbara Lalicki, Harriett Barton, Rosemary Brosnan, Meredith Charpentier, Anne Dunn, Dana Hayward, Maggie Herold, Fumi Kosaka, Marisa Miller, Rachel Orr, and Katherine Rogers. I would also like to thank David Black, Joy Tutela, and Alix Reid for their friendship, assistance, and great ideas. My wife, Joann, and my children, Jenny and Colin, are always a source of inspiration, joy, and support. Without them, I could not do my work.

I especially thank April Prince for her devoted efforts and unique contributions. This book would not have been possible without her tireless work, imagination, and creativity.

This is a Don't Know Much About® book.
Don't Know Much About® is the registered trademark
of Kenneth C. Davis.

Don't Know Much About® Planet Earth
Copyright © 2001 by Kenneth C. Davis

Library of Congress Cataloging-in-Publication Data
Davis, Kenneth C.
    Don't know much about planet Earth / by Kenneth C. Davis.
        p.   ˉcm. —(Don't know much)
    ISBN 0-06-028599-0 — ISBN 0-06-028600-8 (lib. bdg.) — ISBN 0-06-440834-5 (pbk.)
    1. Earth—Miscellanea—Juvenile literature. [1. Earth—Miscellanea. 2. Questions and answers.]
I. Title. II. Series.
QB631.4.D38 2001   00-052967
910—dc21   CIP

Design by Charles Yuen
1   2   3   4   5   6   7   8   9   10
❖
First Edition

CONTENTS

INTRODUCTION

Have you ever been lost? Not just confused, but really lost—separated from your parents at the supermarket or at an amusement park or, worse, at the beach? For most of us, the queasy feeling of being lost is one of the worst sensations in the world. (Trust me, it is even worse for the parents!)

Believe it or not, a lot of people are lost all the time. Not separated from their parents, but completely lost when it comes to knowing where they are in the world. Too many of us don't know Austria from Australia, Belize from Belgium, or the difference between ozone and a no parking zone.

That's why I love maps—maps of the subway system; hiking trail maps; floor plans of museums; maps of America, the world, outer space. I love to look at maps, study them, and know where I am and where I am going. It's fun. Besides, if you always know where you are, nobody can ever tell you to "get lost."

Don't Know Much About® *Planet Earth* is about knowing where we are, how we got there, and where we might be going. That's what geography means. It isn't just memorizing the state capitals or being able to find the Mississippi River. Geography lets us discover the world the way an explorer does. It opens up the whole planet and lets us see extraordinary, far-off places, meet all sorts of interesting people, and understand why the world works the way it does. *Don't Know Much About*® *Planet Earth* is a fun and fascinating way to get to explore the world, only without all those nasty insects buzzing around your ears. So I do hope you lose yourself—in this book!

CHAPTER 1

WHAT'S SO SPECIAL ABOUT EARTH?

What in the world is geography?

Geography is the science that explains why you—yes, you reading this book—are where you are. It asks and answers some of humankind's most basic questions: Where am I? What's over there? How did it get there? What is it like? Why is it there?

Geography is the big mixing bowl of the sciences: it brings together all sorts of other specialties. If you combine a little history, geology, meteorology, biology, economics, astronomy, and almost every other "ology," "onomy," or "omics" you can think of, you'll begin to see what geographers do. They study how we shape—and are shaped by—the shape of the world.

Has Earth always been around?

It has always been a fairly round planet. (It does bulge a little in the middle.) But Earth hasn't always been around. Earth and its neighboring planets started out as a huge cloud of space dust and gas. Then, about 4.6 billion years ago, something—maybe a shock wave from a nearby exploding star—gave the cloud a push, and it began spinning into a flat disk. Gravity pulled some of the dust and gas toward the disk's center. There it clumped into a dense and intensely hot ball of gases and the Sun was born. Most of the other dust and gas formed smaller, cooler clumps that became Earth and the other planets, moons, asteroids, and comets that travel around the Sun as our solar system.

What's so special about Earth?

Of the nine planets in our solar system, Earth is the only one (that we know of) that has life. As the third planet from the Sun, Earth gets just the right amount of heat to keep water in its three forms—liquid, vapor, and ice—and to support our kinds of plants and animals. Earth's atmosphere, the blanket of air that surrounds it, is also unique. It contains oxygen for us to breathe, protects us from the Sun's heat and harmful rays, and keeps our planet warm.

How is Earth like a peach?

Earth might not look or taste like a peach, but the two do have a few things in common. Like a peach, Earth has a thin outer skin. This is Earth's crust. Underneath Earth's crust is the juicy fruit, or mantle. The mantle is a thick layer of really hot rocks and goopy semimelted rock called magma. Underneath the mantle is the peach pit, Earth's core, a solid, superhot ball of iron. Now imagine that the skin of our peachy Earth has been sliced into sixteen or so irregularly shaped pieces. All these separate pieces, or plates, float around the outside of Earth like giant rafts on a sea of molten rock.

230 million years ago, you could have walked from Pole to Pole.

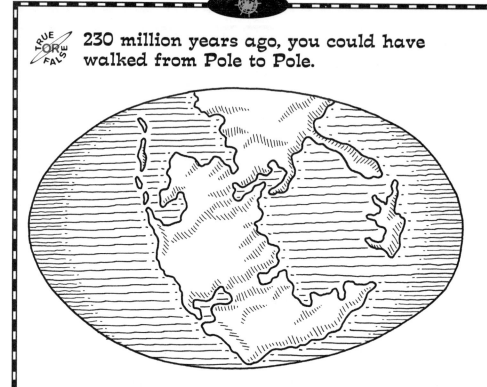

True! Back then, all Earth's land was connected in a huge single mass called Pangaea ("all land" in Greek). So what happened between then and now? Earth's plates have been on the move in a process called plate tectonics. Even though most plates move only a few inches a year, those few inches add up over millions of years. In time, continental drift tore Pangaea apart to form the continents and islands we know today. If you look closely at a map of the world, you can see how the edges of some continents, such as South America and Africa, could still fit together like the pieces of a jigsaw puzzle.

The continents continue to move, about 1/3 inch to 6 inches (3/4 cm to 15 cm) a year. In another few million years, East Africa will probably break off from the rest of Africa, and Mexico's Baja California peninsula will detach from North America.

Earth's plates drift around so slowly that we usually don't know they're moving. But where plates grind into each other or pull apart, there are scenes of slow violence. Sometimes this violence bursts onto Earth's surface when earthquakes rattle our houses, volcanoes erupt, or mountains rise from flat land.

Does everyone agree that there are seven continents?

No. A continent is simply defined as one of the main landmasses on the planet. This definition is a problem when you look at Europe and Asia, because they're one big landmass. That's why some geographers say Europe and Asia are one continent, Eurasia, so that there are only six continents, not seven. (We'll discuss this more in Chapter 6.) But since continents are a way to help us organize and refer to the world's many different lands and peoples, it's usually more useful to say there are seven: Asia, Africa, North America, South America, Antarctica, Europe, and Australia.

Whose fault are earthquakes, anyway?

If you asked the ancient Japanese, they'd blame the thrashing namazu, a giant catfish believed to live underground. Sound a little fishy? Middle Eastern tribes were sure the shaking of Earth was a sign of God's displeasure. Today we know that earthquakes happen after Earth's plates build up pressure by pushing into or squeezing past each other. When the plates can't take the pressure anymore, they release the stress by slipping suddenly along faults, or cracks in Earth's surface. When the rocks along a fault move quickly, they send out ripples, or shock waves, through the ground. The ground moves up and down and side to side, turning what once seemed like a solid surface into a bowl of quivering Jell-O.

Do high tides bring high tidal waves?

A tidal wave is more properly called a tsunami, which is a Japanese word for "harbor wave." Tsunamis have nothing to do with tides, but a lot to do with earthquakes. Quakes under the ocean floor can create these enormous, fast-moving waves that can travel great distances and crash down on people and cities along the coast.

Naturally Extraordinary:

Some Major Earthquakes in World History

1202 Eastern Mediterranean

A severe quake struck from Syria to Egypt, destroying cities in Israel, Syria, and Lebanon. Some sources estimate 1.1 million deaths, which would be more than any other earthquake disaster in history.

1556 Shaanxi Province, China

This deadly quake killed approximately 830,000 people.

1737 Calcutta, India

A large quake in densely populated Calcutta killed about 300,000.

1755 Lisbon, Portugal

One of the most severe urban quakes ever recorded leveled the city and killed as many as 60,000. Shocks were felt as far away as southern France, North Africa, and even the United States.

1811–1812 New Madrid, Missouri, United States

The greatest series of quakes to hit the lower forty-eight states claimed no lives since few people lived in the area. The earthquakes were felt over two-thirds of the United States. They made waves flow backward up the Mississippi River and changed the course of the river in several places.

1923 Honshu Island, Japan

Three shocks of 8.3 on the Richter scale hit the main island of Japan. The cities of Tokyo and Yokohama were nearly destroyed by the earthquake and resulting fires, leaving about 140,000 dead and 1 million homeless.

1950 Assam, India

One of the most violent quakes in modern times, measuring 8.7 on the Richter scale, killed approximately 20,000 to 30,000 people. Explosions and earsplitting noises came from the collapsing underground rock.

1960 Concepción, Chile

In the strongest quake ever recorded—a 9.6 on the Richter scale—the Chilean city was destroyed for the sixth time by earthquakes. Thousands died, and tsunamis killed people in Hawaii, Japan, and the Philippines.

1964 near Anchorage, Alaska, United States

The strongest quake to hit North America measured a whopping 9.2 on the Richter scale and killed about 120 people. The quake was felt around the world, and tsunamis traveled as far as the coast of Antarctica.

1976 Tangshan, China

The deadliest quake in the twentieth century was an 8.2 on the Richter scale. It killed at least 250,000 people.

1988 Armenia

A quake measuring 6.9 on the Richter scale killed almost 25,000 and left another 400,000 homeless. Many were killed by the collapse of large, concrete apartment buildings in the region's densely populated cities.

1990 Northern Iran

An earthquake measuring 7.7 destroyed towns and villages around the Caspian Sea, leaving 50,000 dead and 400,000 homeless.

2001 Gujarat, India

A quake measuring 7.9 on the Richter scale hit western India but was felt across Pakistan, Bangladesh, and Nepal. At least 30,000 were killed and 60,000 wounded, many in the collapse of high-rise buildings that had not been constructed to withstand earthquakes. One million people were left homeless.

Does the Richter scale tell how much an earthquake weighs?

No. The Richter scale measures the energy released by an earthquake. The scale starts at zero and goes up to 9.0. The weakest quakes noticed by people measure around 3.0 on the scale. At 5.0 walls may crack and objects will fall off shelves; from 6.0 to 6.9 large quakes can cause serious damage in populated areas; from 7.0 to 7.9 major quakes cause immense damage; and 8.0 or above measures great earthquakes causing total destruction.

Do people get swallowed by the earth during an earthquake?

Almost never. It's very unlikely that the earth will open up, wait for people to fall in, and close up again. In all of recorded history, it's happened only once, to a woman in Japan in 1948. (It also happened to a cow in San Francisco in 1906.) Most victims of earthquakes die when buildings collapse on top of them or from fires that sweep through the area after the quake.

Do sleeping volcanoes snore?

Sleeping volcanoes don't snore, but sometimes they wake up. Sleeping, or dormant, volcanoes are those that haven't been erupting recently. Of the approximately 2,500 volcanoes on the planet, most are either dormant or extinct (no longer active). Most of Earth's 1,500 or so active volcanoes are along the Ring of Fire that circles the Pacific Ocean.

"A dense, black cloud was coming up behind us, spreading over the Earth like a flood. Darkness fell as if the lamp had been put out in a closed room. The buildings were shaking as if they were being torn from their foundations. Ashes were falling hotter and thicker, followed by bits of pumice and blackened stones, charred and cracked by the flames. . . . I had the belief that the whole world was dying and I with it until a yellowish sun finally revealed a landscape buried deep in ashes like snowdrifts."

—The Roman statesman Pliny the Younger describes the scene witnessed at age seventeen when, during his stay in a town across the Bay of Naples, Mount Vesuvius erupted in A.D. 79.

The Ring of Fire is a long narrow belt of volcanic and earthquake activity around the edge of the Pacific Ocean. It occurs where the plates under the Pacific rub against plates holding North and South America, Australia, and East Asia. The Ring is home to most of Earth's active volcanoes and to many of its worst earthquakes. It also rubs shoulders with some of Earth's most populated areas. In eastern China, Japan, eastern Russia, Oceania, Alaska, or the west coast of the Americas, there's no telling when the ground will shake, rattle and blow.

(N)aturally Extraordinary:

Major Volcanic Eruptions in World History

Around 1480 B.C. Thera, Mediterranean Sea

A powerful eruption destroyed part of the island of Thera (sometimes called Santorini), leaving a crater more than 1,000 feet (305 m) deep. The ash, rains, and tsunami that resulted from this eruption may have destroyed the great civilization on the nearby island of Crete and given rise to the legend of Atlantis, the island destroyed by the gods.

A.D. 79 Mount Vesuvius, Italy

If you've ever heard of the lost city of Pompeii, Mount Vesuvius is the reason. The eruption of Vesuvius buried the Roman city and its neighbor, Herculaneum. More than 16,000 people were suffocated by volcanic gases and buried alive by volcanic ash and rock. When Pompeii was finally dug out in 1749, the city's artifacts and inhabitants were almost perfectly preserved by the ash that covered them. Today you can walk through parts of the city that have been uncovered.

1815 Mount Tambora, Indonesia

When Mount Tambora erupted in one of the largest volcanic blasts ever recorded, the sky turned black with ash and stayed that way for three days. A whole year later, the ash cloud still blocked the sunlight, creating a "Year Without Summer" as far away as New England and Canada. Snow and frost were common even in June, July, and August. About 90,000 people died, most from starvation and disease caused by the destruction.

1883 Krakatau, Indonesia

Three volcanoes that made up the Indonesian island of Krakatau blew up in the largest eruption in modern history. Not only did the eruption cause 130-foot tsunamis that drowned about 36,000 people in Indonesia, it also sent a cloud of dust and ash around Earth several times. The sound of the explosion was heard nearly 3,000 miles (4,828 km) away, making it the loudest sound in recorded history.

1980 Mount St. Helens, United States

The 1980 eruption of Washington State's Mount St. Helens was its first in 123 years. The force of the eruption was so great that the north side of the mountain was blown completely off. Only 61 humans—but millions of plants and animals—were killed. Today the area is making an amazing comeback. Trees and other plants as well as insects, fish, birds, elk, and other animals are already returning to the mountain.

1985 Nevado del Ruiz, Colombia

Melted ice, rock, and ash from an eruption on this snowy volcano turned into deadly lahars, or landslides. The slides buried a town at the volcano's base and killed more than 23,000 people.

How can you tell how old a mountain is?

By its shape. The longer a mountain range has been around, the smoother and rounder its peaks are. Over time, the jagged edges are eroded, or worn away by wind, rain, and ice. Asia's Himalaya Mountains, relatively young, are still rough and craggy. The Appalachian Mountains in eastern North America are a much older, gently rolling range that may once have looked like the Himalayas.

Naturally Extraordinary:

The Highest Mountain Peaks on Each Continent

There are mountains on every continent, and even on much of the ocean floor. In fact, the world's tallest mountain is in the Pacific Ocean: Hawaii's volcanic Mauna Kea rises 33,476 feet (10,203 m) from the ocean floor. However, it isn't considered the world's tallest peak because only 13,796 feet (4,205 m) of it is visible above the water.

The Himalayas hold most of the world's tallest peaks: A list of the ten highest mountains would include nine from that range. Here are the highest peaks on each continent:

Peak	Continent	Country	Elevation
Everest	Asia	China and Nepal	29,035 feet (8,848 m)
Aconcagua	South America	Argentina	22,834 feet (6,960 m)
McKinley	North America	Alaska, USA	20,320 feet (6,194 m)
Kilimanjaro	Africa	Tanzania	19,340 feet (5,895 m)
El'brus	Europe	Russia	18,510 feet (5,642 m)
Vinson Massif	Antarctica		16,067 feet (4,897 m)
Kosciuszko	Australia		7,310 feet (2,228 m)

Why does Earth look mostly blue from outer space?

Because more than two-thirds of the "Blue Planet" is covered with water. So it's kind of funny that Earth is named for its land. Water is where all life started billions of years ago. About 97 percent of all living matter on Earth is in the ocean. Scientists think that today, in the depths of the ocean, there might be ten million species we've never seen.

POP QUIZ: How many oceans are there?

a. one

b. fifty-three

c. four

d. seven

If you said "a," you're correct. But if you said "c," you're also correct. If you look at a globe, you'll see that all the world's oceans are connected—they're part of the same huge body of water. But to make our lives easier, four large sections of that one body of water have been given four different names: Pacific, Atlantic, Indian, and Arctic.

The world's oceans: Who am I?

- I'm the largest of the oceans—in fact, I cover more area than all Earth's land put together! I'm also the deepest ocean, and I'm home to the Mariana Trench, the lowest point on Earth at 35,827 feet (10,920 m) below sea level. I have lots of small islands, many of them volcanic (think Ring of Fire). I was named by the explorer Ferdinand Magellan because of the peaceful weather he encountered in my waters. (He was lucky not to run into my typhoons.) *Pacific*

- I'm the world's second-largest ocean. Much of world's shipping happens on me because I sit between Europe and Africa on one side and the Americas on the other. Most of the world's fish are caught in my waters. I'm less salty than the other oceans because so many big rivers empty into me. *Atlantic*

- I'm the third-largest ocean. Nearly all of me lies south of the equator. Many island nations are found among my waters. *Indian*

- I'm the smallest and shallowest ocean. I'm at the top of the world, and most of me is frozen all year round. *Arctic*

Are the oceans and the Moon in love?

They haven't said, but one thing's for certain: there's definitely an attraction between them, and the Moon is playing hard to get. That's why the oceans have tides. About every twelve hours, the water level in the ocean rises and falls. This happens because the ocean water is attracted to the Moon's (and to a lesser degree, the Sun's) gravity. When the Moon is directly overhead, the water underneath is pulled toward it. This is called high tide. A similar bulge, or high tide, happens on the opposite side of Earth. Low tide occurs in the ocean between each of these bulges.

Are there rivers in the oceans?

Yes! They're called currents. Currents are streams of water that flow along or under the surface of the oceans, the way rivers flow on land. These oceanic rivers help to mix up warm and cold temperatures in the ocean and affect the climate on land and life in the water.

Cold currents bring cool, dry weather to the coastlines they pass. Currents that are warm bring warm, wet weather to the land. One of Earth's major weather patterns is El Niño, caused by the change in currents off the west coast of South America. El Niño is especially strong about once every decade, usually in December. (That's where the name El Niño, for the Christ Child, came from.) But El Niño doesn't come bearing gifts or goodwill. Instead, it replaces cold coastal waters with warm currents, which causes strange weather that can result in lots of damage by floods, droughts, and hurricanes. Though El Niño flows from the eastern Pacific, it can affect weather on three-quarters of the globe.

Who owns the oceans?

Countries that touch the ocean have total control of the waters for 12 miles (19 km) off their own shores. They have economic control (such as fishing and oil exploration rights) out to 200 miles (322 km). Past that, it's no man's land. Why does it matter who owns the oceans? Because there are oil deposits and lots of valuable minerals under them, and everyone wants to know whose they are.

What were the seven seas?

Sailors hundreds of years ago named seven seas that we now know as oceans or parts of oceans. Those seas were called the Arctic, Indian, North Pacific, South Pacific, North Atlantic, South Atlantic, and Antarctic Seas. In those days, if you'd sailed the seven seas, you'd sailed around the world. Mapmakers today still give the name "sea" to many sections of the oceans, as well as to large bodies of water partially or wholly enclosed by land. Some famous seas are the Sea of Japan (an arm of the Pacific Ocean) and the Mediterranean Sea (mostly inside land, but connected to the Atlantic).

How can a sea be a lake?

Basically the same way you can drive on a parkway and park on a driveway—somewhere along the line, the Naming Fairy got confused.

A lake is any body of water enclosed by land. Lake water is usually fresh, not salty. However, the world's largest lake is an enclosed, but salty, body of water in southwest Asia called the Caspian Sea. The world's largest freshwater lake is Lake Superior, one of North America's five Great Lakes. The world's deepest lake is Lake Baikal, in northern Russia. It contains more water than all five of the Great Lakes combined!

Is the Dead Sea dead?

Aside from the fact that the Dead Sea isn't a sea at all (it's another one of those lakes with confusing names), the body of water definitely deserves its name. It is dead, dead, dead. Almost nothing can survive in its waters because the "sea" is so salty. The salt comes from minerals around the sea, and because no river drains the Dead Sea, the salt has nowhere to go. In the area's hot climate, water evaporates quickly and leaves even more salt in the water that remains. (The water is so salty, in fact, that swimmers float easily in it.) If all that lifelessness didn't make you feel low enough, the shore of the Dead Sea also happens to be the lowest point of dry land on Earth's surface.

Why is a strait such an important gate?

A strait is a narrow channel of water that connects two larger bodies of water. Many straits are strategically important trade and travel routes. Those who control a strait decide whose ships can go in and out. That's a lot of power. (Imagine that there's only one route to your school lunchroom. You could make a lot of money if you controlled that route.)

The Strait of Gibraltar, which links the Mediterranean Sea and the Atlantic Ocean, is one of the most famous straits. It is a gateway to the cities and cultures of the Mediterranean. Another strait that has been important in recent years is the Strait of Hormuz, connecting the Persian Gulf to the Indian Ocean. Many countries around the Persian Gulf export oil, which is most often shipped through the strait. If those countries can't get their oil out through the waterway, they lose a lot of money, and the importing countries are left without fuel.

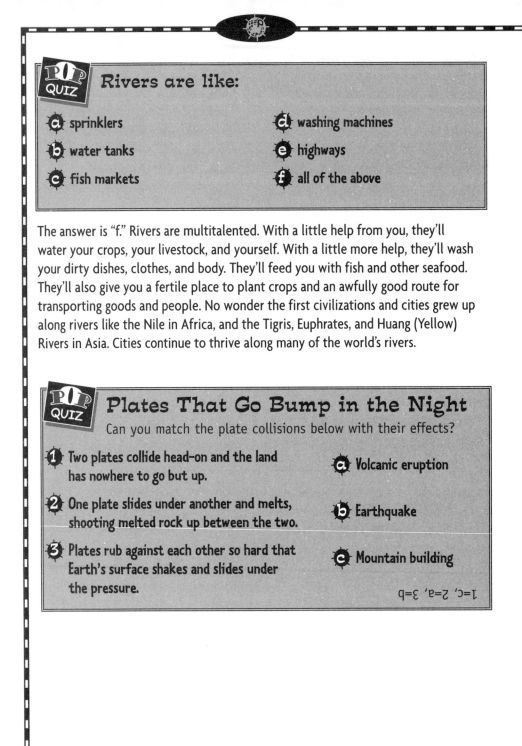

POP QUIZ — Rivers are like:

a sprinklers

b water tanks

c fish markets

d washing machines

e highways

f all of the above

The answer is "f." Rivers are multitalented. With a little help from you, they'll water your crops, your livestock, and yourself. With a little more help, they'll wash your dirty dishes, clothes, and body. They'll feed you with fish and other seafood. They'll also give you a fertile place to plant crops and an awfully good route for transporting goods and people. No wonder the first civilizations and cities grew up along rivers like the Nile in Africa, and the Tigris, Euphrates, and Huang (Yellow) Rivers in Asia. Cities continue to thrive along many of the world's rivers.

POP QUIZ — Plates That Go Bump in the Night

Can you match the plate collisions below with their effects?

1 Two plates collide head-on and the land has nowhere to go but up.

2 One plate slides under another and melts, shooting melted rock up between the two.

3 Plates rub against each other so hard that Earth's surface shakes and slides under the pressure.

a Volcanic eruption

b Earthquake

c Mountain building

1=c, 2=a, 3=b

CHAPTER 2

HOW ARE DESERTS LIKE DESSERTS?

Do meteorologists study meteors?

Not unless one lands on their weather station. The term "meteor" comes from the Greek word for "in the air." Meteorologists study the atmosphere and the way it behaves— the weather, in other words.

The terms "weather" and "climate" are often confused. If you say a big storm hit and dumped 20 inches (51 cm) of snow on the ground, you're talking about weather. If you say Siberia is cold and snowy all year round, you're describing the area's climate, or weather patterns over time.

Why do Australian kids have to go to school in June, July, and August?

Because they don't go to school in December or January. That's their summer vacation.

Earth circles the Sun at an angle, the way the leaning Tower of Pisa leans. The half that tilts toward the Sun gets more sunlight, so that half is warmer and its season is summer. The half that tilts away gets less sunlight and is experiencing winter. Since Australia is in the southern half, or hemisphere, of the world, its seasons are the opposite of those in North America, Europe, and Asia.

Why don't New York and Madrid have the same weather?

Because the land and water around them are so different. New York and Madrid are the same distance north of the equator, which is an imaginary line that divides the world into northern and southern halves. Still, New York is much wetter and colder than Madrid. That's because climate is affected by all sorts of geographical factors, including the nearness of warm or cold ocean currents, mountain ranges that trap rain or block it, and the direction of steady winds. Climatologists divide the world into climate regions such as tropical, dry, temperate, and polar. Dry climates include a lot of deserts, tropical areas may support rain forests, and temperate regions have milder weather and moderate rainfall.

Where should it be summer vacation all year round?

In the tropics! The area around the equator, called the tropics, gets the most direct sunlight all year long, so it's almost always hot there. Still, kids who live there do go to school, just like kids in milder climates.

If you like to ice-skate in the winter and swim in the summer, where should you live?

In a temperate zone, between the always-warm tropical zone and the always-cold polar zone. Temperate zones, which lie in the middle latitudes, have a change in seasons but rarely get superhot or supercold. Temperate climates are comfortable places to live and are good areas for agriculture and industry. But if you live in places like Japan, Europe, southern Australia, or much of the United States or China, you already know that!

How are deserts like desserts?

Deserts, like apple pie, can be served hot or cold. A desert is any place that receives less than 10 inches (25 cm) of rainfall a year. A desert is always arid, or dry, but it's not necessarily hot. In fact, Antarctica qualifies as a desert because it gets very little snowfall, despite having so much ice on its surface. Most deserts are just north or south of the equator, though, and they are usually hot. Africa's Sahara boasts the highest temperature ever recorded, 136.4°F (58°C).

Since a desert doesn't have to be hot, it also doesn't have to be sandy. (In fact, most aren't.) Even the Sahara is only 30 percent sand. The rest of it is covered with gravel-like rocks. Many deserts have thin, dry dirt, rocks, and scrubby plants.

(N)aturally Extraordinary:

Some Significant Deserts of the World and What Makes Them Cool (or Not)

• Sahara, Northern Africa

The world's largest hot desert has 3,475,000 square miles (8,999,600 sq km) of sand and rock.

• Antarctica

The 5,100,000 square miles (13,208,000 sq km) of the world's largest polar desert are icy but rarely receive snow or rain.

• Gobi, Mongolia and China

The world's second-largest desert is also the most northern.

• Arabian, Arabian Peninsula

The world's largest oil reserves lie beneath this desert.

• Great Australian, Australia

This desert covers about half the continent, including nearly all the interior.

• Mojave, Southern California, United States

America's largest desert is home to Death Valley, the lowest point in the Western Hemisphere and the record holder for North American heat at 134°F (57°C).

• Atacama, Chile

The world's driest desert gets a throat-parching .02 inches of moisture a year.

Should Old MacDonald move to the tropical rain forest?

Not if he wants to keep farming. Tropical rain forests, such as those in South America or Africa, may support many animals and tropical plants,

but they don't make good farmland. The soil of tropical rain forests typically doesn't contain many nutrients. If trees are cut down, the soil becomes even poorer as it is baked by the sun and deprived of falling leaves to enrich it. Farmers who chop down tropical rain forests to make room for farms soon find that the land cannot support them.

The energy released in one day of a hurricane could power the United States for three years.

What's the difference between a tornado, a hurricane, a typhoon, and a cyclone?

A tornado is a whirling column of air that is born from a single huge thundercloud. It can have winds up to 300 miles (483 km) an hour but usually lasts only a few minutes. A hurricane's winds are a little slower, but the storm is much, much bigger than a tornado. Made from many thunderstorms swept together into a huge, circling storm cloud, a hurricane can be 600 miles (966 km) wide. Hurricanes start in the warm waters of the Atlantic, near Africa, and typically move west toward North America. Just to make matters confusing, a hurricane is called a typhoon when it begins in the western Pacific Ocean. Both hurricanes and typhoons are tropical cyclones; a cyclone is any kind of big, circling storm.

As hurricanes form, the World Meteorological Organization names them in alphabetical order. (One is named Arthur, the next Betty, and so on.) All but five letters of the English alphabet (Q, U, X, Y, and Z) are used. The names alternate between male and female so neither gender gets offended.

"We stood at the windows and watched the houses around us break up, wash away, and become battering rams to knock and tear others apart as they were hurled and swept about. The water kept rising; the sounds of the storm were frightening; the house creaked and groaned as if it were in some kind of agony."

—Ruby Credo, survivor of the Galveston, Texas, hurricane of 1900. The most dangerous hurricane ever to hit the United States, the Galveston storm killed more than 6,000 people.

Are wetlands wastelands?

Definitely not, though we once thought they were. Wetlands, also known as swamps, marshes, and bogs, are areas that are covered by water at least part of the year. They're found on every continent except Antarctica; one of the most famous is the Florida Everglades, the largest freshwater marsh in the world. Wetlands are some of the most fertile and productive ecosystems on the planet—they're overflowing with plant, fish, insect, and animal life. They also control water cycles by absorbing flood water. They filter pollution from the water that passes through them.

Coastal wetlands are important nurseries for fish and shellfish, because two-thirds of the fish caught in the world are hatched in their rich, protective tidal zones. But before the 1970s, wetlands were considered wastelands and breeding grounds for pesky insects. Nearly half the wetlands in the United States were filled in or drained to make room for building and farming. Sections of Boston, San Francisco, and Washington, D.C., were built where wetlands used to be. Today, though, we're more careful. Destroying wetlands in the United States and some other parts of the world is illegal.

Why should you hug a tree?

Because trees are our friends. You've heard it before, but it really couldn't be more true. The world's forests have been shrinking ever since people began clearing them for firewood, building materials, and farmland thousands of years ago. Loggers are now chopping away at the tropical rain forests that provide so much of the world's oxygen and plant and animal life. An astounding half—half!—of the world's tropical forests have been destroyed in the past one hundred years. That's like giving Earth an operation to remove one of its lungs.

Cutting trees also contributes to the gradual warming of the planet, or the "greenhouse effect." (So called because, like sunlight in a garden greenhouse, the heat from the Sun's rays gets into Earth's atmosphere and can't get out.) Global warming comes from too much carbon dioxide and other "greenhouse gases" in the atmosphere. When we burn coal and oil for fuel, we release carbon dioxide. Trees take carbon dioxide from the air and turn it into oxygen. So fewer trees means less gas is absorbed, more stays in the atmosphere, and the global thermometer just keeps rising.

If Earth is getting warmer, will we be able to swim at the North Pole?

We won't be able to swim there, but some of the ice at the North and South Poles will probably melt as global warming continues. In fact, some scientists say that the ice at the North Pole is already doing just that.

During the last hundred years, Earth has warmed up slightly. The average sea level has risen about 12 inches (30 cm). Scientists say that by 2100, the average global temperature could rise another 3.5°F. If this happens, some of the water that's now trapped as ice at the North and South Poles will melt, flooding low-lying coastal cities. Some tiny islands in the Republic of the Maldives, in the Indian Ocean, have already been evacuated because of flooding. More than 50 percent of the people in the world, including those in New York, London, and New Orleans, live within 50 miles (80 km) of a coast. They may be the next to feel the effects of global warming.

Global warming might also change the world's climate, bringing drought to some areas and floods to others. Warm climate zones might move north in the Northern Hemisphere and south in the Southern Hemisphere, changing the places where crops can grow and displacing farmers. Plants and animals would be affected, too, and possibly suffer through a period of extinctions.

What happens if we use up all the world's coal, oil, and natural gas?

There won't be any more for a long, long time. These fossil fuels, so named because they are made from the fossil remains of once-living plants and animals, are nonrenewable resources—once they're used up, we won't find any more.

Forests, on the other hand, are a renewable resource because they can be replanted. We can also create energy from wind power, solar power (from the Sun), hydroelectric power (from falling water), geothermal power (from heat within Earth), nuclear power (from the splitting of atoms), and biomass power (from wood, leaves, and other parts of plants). As we use up more of the world's nonrenewable resources, these alternatives will become more and more important. Equally crucial is conservation, or the practice of saving natural resources for future generations. Reduce, reuse, and recycle!

Is there enough food to feed the world?

The world can feed itself, yet about 24,000 people around the world die of hunger every day. That's one person every 3.6 seconds. Why does this happen? One reason is Earth's booming population. The world held 2.5 billion people in 1950 and 6 billion in 2000. It is projected to contain 10 billion or more of us by 2050. Another reason is that even though it's a big planet, most of its people are concentrated in the few places where they can grow and transport food easily—typically in mild, lowland regions along rivers and coasts. The world's food and resources just aren't evenly spread out, and the places that are blessed with fertile land don't always want to share their food with places that aren't. But there is hope. New kinds of seeds, fertilizers, and farming methods are being introduced, and crops are getting a little better. But the improvements of this Green Revolution require money and education to set up—in precisely the places that don't have much of either.

CHAPTER 3

WHY ARE MAPS SO POWERFUL?

TRUE OR FALSE **The Italian explorer Christopher Columbus proved that the world was round.**

False. That was old news in Chris's day. Way back in the fourth century B.C., the Greek philosopher Aristotle knew that Earth must be round because he saw that the planet cast a curved shadow on the Moon during an eclipse. Before Aristotle, many Greek philosophers had thought that Earth was flat, a disk floating in an endless ocean or hanging freely in space.

Why can't you use a camel during a math test?

Because—little did you know—camels can be used as calculators. More than 2,000 years ago, a Greek librarian named Eratosthenes (276–196 B.C.) used a camel to help him measure the circumference of, or distance around, Earth.

Eratosthenes heard of a well in Syene (in what is now Aswan, Egypt) in which the Sun's reflection could be seen on June 21, the longest day of the year. Eratosthenes figured that meant the Sun was directly over the well on that day. He also knew that

Syene was pretty much due south of the city of Alexandria. By measuring the shadow cast by an obelisk (a tall carved stone) in Alexandria on June 21, the librarian computed the length of two sides of a right triangle—the length of the shadow and the height of the obelisk. Then he figured the angle of the remaining side of the triangle—about 7 degrees, or 1/50 of a full circle—and knew that was how far the Sun was from being directly overhead in Alexandria.

Now, here's where the camel came in. Eratosthenes learned that it took a camel fifty days to travel from Alexandria to Syene. Since the average well-fed camel could cover 100 stadia a day (stadia were an ancient measurement of the length of a Greek racecourse), the distance between the two cities was 5,000 stadia. Multiplying that distance by 50 (the portion of the circle he calculated using the obelisk), he came up with a circumference of 250,000 stadia for Earth. That's equivalent to 25,000 miles (40,233 km). It's also amazingly close to Earth's actual circumference of 24,901 miles (40,073 km) at the equator.

Though the earliest humans surely wondered about their world, it was the librarian Eratosthenes who actually coined the word geography (from "geo," meaning the earth, and "graphy," meaning written description).

Why are the countries around the Mediterranean Sea called "the cradle of civilization"?

Because so many of ancient history's rich, powerful, and influential nations grew up there thousands of years ago. The Sumerians, Babylonians, Egyptians, Greeks, Romans, and others all became great in lands around the protected waters of the Mediterranean Sea. Other significant civilizations existed in Africa and Asia around the same time, but it was mainly the people of the Mediterranean who explored the world to create the maps we know today.

Exploration often went hand in hand with conquest. The Macedonian general Alexander the Great (356–323 B.C.) conquered an empire that stretched from Greece to India. (All before he died at age thirty-three!) With him traveled geographers, scientists, architects, an official historian, and bematists, or people who measured distances by counting their steps. Together they mapped thousands of miles of territory unknown to westerners.

Why did Columbus sail west to go east?

Not because he had no sense of direction. While some explorers were trying to sail all the way around Africa to get to the rich trade routes of Asia, others thought there must be an easier way. "Sail west to get to the east!" said these bold thinkers. Since the world is round, it would have worked, if two big unknown continents—the Americas—hadn't been in the way.

Columbus never would have guessed that two large continents and the vast Pacific Ocean lay between him and China. That's because he thought the world was smaller than it actually was. About 300 years after Eratosthenes calculated the distance around Earth, a great geographer named Ptolemy (c. A.D. 100–170) used different (and wrong) calculations from the Greek geographer Strabo that misled sailors for more than 1,000 years. His new measurements shrunk the planet by a quarter to about 18,000 miles, so Columbus didn't think he had as far to sail.

Are a country, a nation, and a state the same thing?

Nope. They're all a little different. Here's the lowdown: A country usually means the territory of, or land that belongs to, a nation. A nation is generally a large group of people who live under a single, usually independent, government. The group often shares a similar culture, history, language, and similar customs. Most nations, but not all, have a country. (That's why countries are also called nations.) At the same time, many countries are home to more than one nation. The largest nation without a country are the Kurds, who are scattered around eastern Europe and the Middle East. Just to confuse you, a state can be either a nation (like the State of Israel), or just one political unit of a nation (like the fifty states in the United States of America).

People drew maps before they wrote words.

True. Though we don't have proof, the earliest humans probably scratched symbols in the dust to show their friends where to catch the fattest fish and gather the nicest nuts. The oldest map we know of is a clay tablet from Babylonia (present-day northern Iraq). Made in about 2300 B.C., it showed the city of Lagash. The Babylonians and the Egyptians also made early maps of their lands, which they used to set property taxes.

Polynesian navigators sailed for thousands of miles among the many islands in the Pacific more than 3,000 years ago. These great sailors made maps of tied palm fibers and shells. Palms showed wave patterns; shells were islands.

GEOGRAPHIC VOICES

"You've got to be careful if you don't know where you are going, because you may not get there."

—Yogi Berra (1925–), American baseball player

These earliest maps were local maps. The first known world map arrived on the scene in about 600 B.C. It's another Babylonian tablet, about the size of a computer disk, that shows a circle with two lines running through it. The circle was Earth, and the two lines were the Tigris and Euphrates Rivers. The whole circle is surrounded by the "world ocean." To the map's maker, that was the whole world.

What is this a map of?

Gotcha! It's a map of North and South America. Why is it upside down? Only because you're used to seeing maps with north at the top. We've been showing the world that way ever since Ptolemy first did it around A.D. 130. (Yes, that's the same Ptolemy who shrunk Earth with his incorrect calculations.) So today we take it for granted that north is at the top, but if Ptolemy had put south at the top of maps, maybe we would do that today. Mapmakers probably also put north at the top because the needle of a magnetic compass, invented in China about A.D. 1,000, always points north in the Northern Hemisphere.

Maps and What We Use Them for: A Matching Game

Maps are fabulous tools that can give us all sorts of information. For example, say you're going to open a ski resort that you hope will be very successful. Before you start construction, you might want to pull out a few maps.

1 Physical map

2 Political map

3 Climate map

4 Population/distribution map

5 Road map

a shows an area's climate, its weather patterns over time. Will people want to ski where it's hot, rainy, or always cloudy?

b otherwise known as an "impossible-to-fold" map, this shows the roads that could lead to your resort.

c shows how many of something—people, pizza parlors, dog groomers—are in an area. Use this to make sure there will not be too many other ski resorts near yours.

d outlines the boundaries, or borders, between countries and states and shows cities. Use this to find out in what state and near which cities you should put your resort.

e shows Earth's natural features, like mountains and valleys. Use this to figure out where it's hilly enough to build your resort.

Once your resort is up and running (in the perfect place, thanks to all the maps you consulted), you'll probably want to make your own map of your resort. Skiers will want to know which runs are which, so they don't mistake expert slopes for the bunny hill. You'll also want them to know where the lodges are so they can buy lots of hot cocoa.

1=e, 2=d, 3=a, 4=c, 5=b

Why are maps so powerful?

Maps pack lots of useful information into a small space. They help doctors trace the source of a disease. They lead fire trucks to the right address. They bring lost hikers out of the woods. Maps can also make you rich and famous. They might take you to a pirate's buried treasure, or to something even more valuable. In the fifteenth century, maps of the newly explored West African coastline were considered so precious that Portugal's government forbade, under penalty of death, the selling of any of those maps to foreigners.

World of WORDS

A book of maps is called an atlas, after a character in Greek mythology who held the sky on his shoulders. Atlas was often pictured on ancient books and maps.

Anatomy of a Map

A map is a drawing, or representation, of a place. An accurate map must be drawn to scale. That means that if the shopping mall is twice as far away from your house as the park is, then it should be shown that way on the map. A map of your neighborhood would have a small scale, where an inch might equal half a mile. A globe that shows the world has a large scale, where an inch might equal about 660 miles. (That's 42 million times smaller than Earth!) The map scale, which usually looks like a little ruler in one corner of the map, tells you the real distances between the places shown on the map.

The compass rose shows the cardinal, or main, directions of a compass: north, south, east, and west. It will show you how these directions relate to the places on your map. North (N) almost always points to the top of the map, with west (W) to the left, east (E) to the right, and south (S) to the bottom. You can remember where east and west belong on a compass rose, because when they're in the right places, they spell "WE."

A map's legend, or key, tells you what the map's symbols mean. A star might be a capital city, or a tent might be a campground.

Why will maps of the world always, always, always be wrong?

Because they're flat, and Earth is round. If you peel an orange and try to lay the skin flat, you'll see why you can't flatten out a sphere. Pretend the orange is Earth. Cut from the North to the South Poles through the peel. Now try to take off the peel and lay it flat. The peel breaks apart and won't lie down. Some aspect of the land masses on a flat world map—distance, shape, size—is always wrong.

The best way to truly represent Earth is as a round globe. Globes aren't always practical, however. You can't fold them up and fit them in the glove compartment, you can't put them in a book, and you can't get one nearly big enough to show important things like how to get from your house to the nearest ice cream parlor. Maps are much more convenient.

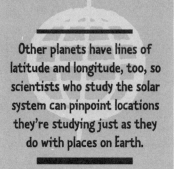

Other planets have lines of latitude and longitude, too, so scientists who study the solar system can pinpoint locations they're studying just as they do with places on Earth.

The most common solution to the problem of showing the round world on a flat piece of paper is to draw the map according to a particular projection. One of the most famous of these is called the Mercator projection. Back in the 1500s, a mapmaker named Gerardus Mercator tried to map the world more accurately by doing some cutting and pasting. To make the shapes of the oceans and continents correct, Mercator split the oceans in half and stretched the land at the North and South Poles so it looks a lot bigger than it really is. (On a Mercator projection, Greenland looks bigger than South America. In reality, South America is eight times larger than Greenland.)

What was the first World Wide Web?

Lines of latitude and longitude. These lines were first used about 2,000 years ago when Greek geographers divided Earth into sections by running a bunch of imaginary lines horizontally and vertically around the planet. Today's mapmakers still use these lines, which let us pinpoint any place on Earth.

Lines of latitude are those that run around Earth sideways. (These lines are also called parallels because they're parallel to each other—they never meet.) Lines of longitude run up and down (north and south) around Earth, getting closer together at the poles.

Latitude is divided into 180 degrees. Zero degrees latitude is at the equator, the imaginary line that runs around the center of Earth. The North Pole is 90 degrees north latitude, and the South Pole is 90 degrees south latitude.

TRUE OR FALSE There are 60 minutes in a degree.

True! But don't worry. That doesn't mean there aren't 60 minutes in an hour, too. Like clockmakers, mapmakers use "minutes" to divide units into smaller parts. Map minutes divide each degree of latitude. We need minutes because there are only 180 degrees of latitude, which means there are still 69 miles (111 km) between degrees. Sometimes even minutes aren't precise enough, so minutes are divided into . . . you guessed it, seconds. By using degrees, minutes, and seconds, you can pinpoint any place on Earth to within 100 feet (30.5 m).

If you lose a day, where should you go to find it?

To the international date line. The international date line is an imaginary line in the middle of the Pacific Ocean at about 180 degrees longitude. It separates one day from the next. The international date line is halfway around the globe from the prime meridian, or the line chosen to be the zero line for longitude. The prime meridian runs through Greenwich, England.

What day it is depends on which side of the international date line you're on. If you're on the west side, it's one day later than if you're on the east side, no matter what time of day or night it is. If it's noon on Tuesday on the east side, and you step over to the west, your local time will now be noon on Wednesday. So if you cross the line from east to west, you lose a day. But don't worry. You'll find it again when you cross the line from west to east. Do that on your birthday, and you get to celebrate twice!

Why isn't it the same time at the same time all over the world?

It seems like it would be easiest to set one World Clock for the whole planet to follow. But that would probably make lots of people pretty confused, since we all like our clocks to match the Sun, no matter where on Earth we are. When the Sun is directly above our heads, we say it's noon. But since Earth spins, the Sun is directly above different places at different times. So in the 1870s, a clever Canadian named Sanford Fleming came up with a timely solution. He proposed dividing Earth into twenty-four time zones that are 15 degrees of longitude apart, one for each hour of the day.

People working at the North and South Poles use Universal Coordinated Time, which is the time at Greenwich, England. Otherwise their work areas would be divided into twenty-four very tiny time zones where the lines of longitude come together.

In 1884, people attending a world conference on time zones agreed to adopt Fleming's system. Although many countries have adapted the system slightly (China, for instance, maintains a single time zone), in general it works around the world. When it's 12 noon in Chicago, it's 7 P.M. in Paris and 1 A.M. in Bangkok.

How do people make maps of places no one's ever been?

Mapmaking today is a whole different ball game from when Columbus went exploring. Maps of his day and before were based on the drawings and reports of explorers. But the mapmakers also used lots of guesswork to fill in the blanks. If there was an empty spot on a map, the mapmakers filled it in with whatever they wanted. Sometimes they included sea monsters and other crazy creatures.

Maps became more accurate when land surveyors were sent out to measure distances and take detailed notes. Even better were maps made from airplanes, using aerial photographs to show the lay of the land from above.

But today we can top even that. Cartographers, or mapmakers, can map out every nook and cranny of a place without anyone ever coming near it. How? They use satellites that look at Earth from outer space. Satellites photograph Earth using many wavelengths of light, including some, such as infrared, that we can't see with our eyes. They also use radar to sense the height and shape of objects on the ground. They can tell the exact height of mountains and show us the depths of the ocean floor. Right now, there are dozens of satellites taking pictures of Earth. Smile!

What's left to explore?

Earth has many nooks and crannies, like remote caves, that haven't been fully explored, but the real final frontier for our planet is the ocean. Hidden in the dark, protected by the crushing pressure of tons of water, the depths of the ocean are still a mystery to us. Yet there are 40,000 miles of mountain ranges on the ocean floor, enormous canyons that drop miles into Earth's crust, bizarre animals around hot mineral vents—and more. Our ocean planet still has plenty of mysteries. So does the sky. Humans have always been curious about the stars and heavens. Geography itself began with attempts to understand the universe and Earth's place in it. (In fact, astronomy is called the first science.)

Back in 1500, a Chinese scientist named Wan Hu tied forty-seven gunpowder rockets to a wicker chair in an attempt to build a flying machine. (He died when it exploded.) It wasn't until the middle of the twentieth century that we had the technology to move into space. Yet walking on the moon in 1969 was, as Neil Armstrong said, just a "small step." Much remains to be learned, understood, and discovered about our vast universe.

GEOGRAPHIC VOICES

"Suddenly from behind the rim of the Moon . . . there emerges a sparkling blue and white jewel, a light, delicate blue sphere laced with slowly swirling veils of white, rising like a small pearl in a thick sea of black mystery. It takes more than a moment to fully realize this is Earth . . . home."

—Edgar Mitchell, U.S. astronaut, 1971

CHAPTER 4

AFRICA

DOES YOUR FAMILY TREE HAVE ITS ROOTS IN AFRICA?

BIGGEST, HIGHEST, DEEPEST . . .

Size

Second-largest continent: 11,609,000 sq mi (30,065,000 sq km)

Highest mountain

Kilimanjaro (in Tanzania): 19,340 ft (5,895 m)

Lowest point

Lake Assal (in Djibouti): 512 ft (156 m) below sea level

Largest lake

Lake Victoria: 26,836 sq mi (69,500 sq km)

Longest river

Nile: 4,241 mi (6,825 km)

Largest desert

Sahara: 3,500,000 sq mi (9,065,000 sq km)

Largest island

Madagascar: 226,658 sq mi (587,000 sq km)

What language should you learn if you're traveling to Africa?

Take your pick—there are more than a thousand different languages and dialects spoken by Africa's many tribal groups. Although it is the only continent without a major mountain range, Africa is a rugged place that's not very easy to get around in. As a result, instead of forming big nations with central governments, people there built lots of separate cultures, laws, and languages around local chiefs. Even today, the second-largest continent has fifty-three countries—far more than any other. Africa also has a wonderful variety of plant and animal life. Its deserts, great open grasslands, and jungles are home to lions, leopards, elephants, giraffes, monkeys, ostriches, and hippos. Yet aside from its great rivers—the Nile and the Congo—Africa doesn't have much water.

Does your family tree have its roots in Africa?

It sure does—just like everyone's. Scientists think that our earliest ancestors—apelike creatures who walked upright and probably used simple tools of rocks and twigs—first appeared in Africa four to five million years ago. Those creatures, called australopithecines ("southern apes"), might have swung through the trees like their primate ancestors, though they probably didn't do that very often.

Why did our ancestors stop swinging and start walking? And why in Africa?

It's all about geography. First, ancient Africa is where primates (the group of animals that includes apes, monkeys, and humans) developed. Second, they lived there when Earth was a much cooler place. Land that is now desert was once savanna, or open grasslands. On the savanna, there weren't many trees to swing from, and standing up made sense. If you wanted to be on the lookout for animals that might eat you, what would you do? You'd stand as tall as you could and gaze over the open fields. And what would you do once you started walking on two legs instead of four, and your hands were free? You'd make tools and weapons to carry with you. That's what set humans apart from other animals.

World of WORDS

The names scientists have given to our various ancestors describe what each of these early humans was like. About 2.5 million years ago, australopithecine evolved into *Homo habilis* ("handy human"), who had a larger brain than australopithecine and made and used simple tools. Then about 1.6 million years ago came *Homo erectus* ("upright human"), who may have stood 6 feet tall. Members of *Homo erectus* made more kinds of tools, built shelters, and used fire to cook and keep warm. They also got adventurous. They were the first of our ancestors to leave Africa and walk to Europe and Asia.

You might think the next species, *Homo sapiens* ("wise human"), got tired of walking and invented the vehicle. But *sapiens*, who developed about 400,000 to 200,000 years ago, wasn't that wise. Clothes, jewelry, and cave paintings, yes; the wheel, no. *Homo sapiens* eventually evolved into a modern form, *Homo sapiens sapiens* ("very wise human"), about 50,000 years ago.

How many miles of Nile are there?

The Nile River in Africa stretches farther than any other river on the planet. Its 4,241 miles (6,825 km) would flow all the way across the United States and halfway back again. You don't have to worry about anyone taking you on a never-ending cruise on the Never-ending Nile, though. The river, like others in Africa, is so hard to travel that no one even went from one end to the other until 1864—even though people had lived along its shores for nearly 7,000 years.

The Nile starts high up in the mountains in East Africa and flows down to the Mediterranean Sea. (On a map, it looks like it's flowing "up," but really it's just flowing north.) Where the Nile empties into the Mediterranean, it branches into many smaller rivers. The Nile and its delta (the fertile land where the river empties into the sea) have been a lifeline in the desert since the beginning of recorded time. The villages that formed on its shores eventually came together to make the great kingdom of Egypt, one of humankind's greatest and longest-lived civilizations. Even today, more than 95 percent of Egypt's population lives within sight of the Nile or its delta.

Naturally Extraordinary:
The World's Longest Rivers

Nile	Africa	4,241 miles (6,825 km)
Amazon	South America	4,000 miles (6,437 km)
Chang Jiang (Yangtze)	Asia	3,964 miles (6,380 km)
Missouri-Mississippi	North America	3,710 miles (5,971 km)
Yenisey-Angara	Asia	3,440 miles (5,536 km)
Huang (Yellow)	Asia	3,395 miles (5,464 km)
Ob-Irtyish	Asia	3,362 miles (5,410 km)

Is sub-Saharan Africa buried under the desert?

Sub-Saharan does mean "below the Sahara," but in the case of Africa it means the countries that are below, or south of, the Sahara. Some forty-six countries and 600 million people make up this varied region.

Geographers sometimes divide Africa into northern and sub-Saharan regions because they are quite different in culture and climate. The countries of North Africa are generally Islamic, and most of their people speak Arabic languages. Their land is dry, dry, dry, dominated by the desert and the need for water. South of the Sahara there is a greater blend of ethnic groups and religions, including Islam, Christianity, and Hinduism. Sub-Saharan Africans speak at least thirteen major languages and thousands of others. Their land is a mixture of tropical grasslands, mountains, rain forests, jungles—almost everything except polar ice.

What does the Sahara Desert eat?

The land around it. Like many of the world's other deserts, the Sahara is expanding around the edges. Many people near the desert, needing food and firewood, overuse the land by growing too many crops or grazing too many cattle or chopping too many trees. Soon there's no grass or trees left to hold the soil in place. It dries up, and the desert moves in. The growth of a desert is called desertification.

World of WORDS

The word "Sahara" comes from the Arabic word for desert, so we're actually calling it the "Desert Desert"!

How do we know the Sahara wasn't always a desert?

The people who lived there thousands of years ago, when the Sahara was a cooler, wetter place, created a whole gallery of rock art that gives us a glimpse of what their lives were like. The earliest art shows crocodiles and giraffes. Later art depicts humans; the elephants, rhinos, and other large animals they hunted; and the cattle they herded.

"Another of their good qualities is their habit of wearing clean, white garments on Fridays. Even if a man has nothing but an old worn shirt, he washes it and cleans it, and wears it to the Friday service. Yet another is their zeal for learning the Koran by heart. They put their children in chains if they show any backwardness in memorizing it, and they are not set free until they have it by heart."

—Ibn Battuta (c. 1304–1374), writing about Muslims he visited in Mali in his book *Travels in Asia and Africa*

Sometimes called the Muslim Marco Polo, Ibn Battuta was the greatest traveler of his day—and perhaps the greatest traveler of all time. Born to a wealthy family in Morocco, in northwest Africa, Ibn Battuta grew up studying the Koran, the holy book of the Islamic religion. As a Muslim, he was required to make one religious journey to the holy city of Mecca. What began as that journey became nearly thirty years of travel through all the Muslim world—North Africa and the Middle East—and beyond. Ibn Battuta ventured as far as China and Russia, seeing more of the known world than any traveler before him. At the very least, he covered 75,000 miles (120,700 km). That's more than most of today's travelers, and they're not traveling in camel caravans.

Who called Africa the "Dark Continent"?

Europeans did. The name didn't mean Africa wasn't sunny; instead, "dark" was another name for mysterious. Until the fifteenth century, Europeans were mainly familiar with the northern part of Africa, where they had been trading for thousands of years. But all the rest of Africa remained a mystery—even its size. Europeans hadn't traveled across the Sahara Desert, nor had they sailed very far south for fear of what they'd find. There were rumors of boiling water and man-eating serpents past the equator.

And yet, Africa was vibrant. Most people know that the Egyptians built some pretty awesome pyramids, but not as many know about Africa's other great kingdoms. Hundreds of years before Columbus sailed the ocean blue, the kingdoms of Mali, Ghana, Songhay, and others were centers of trade, industry, religion, and education. More gold was traded in Ghana than anywhere in the world (giving that region the nickname "Gold Coast"). Songhay had a university and medical school. Music, dance, and art in gold, silver, bronze, and ivory were a vital part of life.

Is Africa's coast a No Parking Zone for boats?

Just about. When Europeans started sailing down Africa's western coast nearly 600 years ago, they rarely stopped on the continent. There was nowhere to drop their anchors. Much of Africa's coast is lined with rocks or cliffs, which don't make good harbors. Where sandy beaches do exist, powerful waves come crashing in. Even when Europeans did find places to stop, they couldn't venture very far into the continent. Africa's rivers are nearly impossible to navigate because they're full of rapids and waterfalls. The deserts, rain forests, and jungles aren't too friendly, either. Even Africans themselves didn't travel much over the rough terrain.

What was Africa's "black gold"?

Its people. When Europeans first began inching down the west coast of Africa, their goal was to find a new route to India. But it didn't take long for them to realize that Africa offered its own riches that were worth stopping for, riches even more valuable than gold. The trade in slaves—black gold—would change the face of the world forever.

Between 1500 and 1850, about 13 million Africans were captured by European slave traders and forced across the ocean to colonies in the Americas. Some African rulers sold their own people or captives from other tribes to European slave traders. Many of Africa's strongest and healthiest people were forced to leave their homes behind.

GEOGRAPHIC VOICES

"One day, when all our people were gone out to their works as usual, and only I and my dear sister were left to mind the house, two men and a woman got over our walls, and in a moment seized us both, and, without giving us time to cry out, or make resistance, they stopped our mouths, and ran off with us into the nearest wood. Here they tied our hands. . . . My cries had no other effect than to make them tie me faster and stop my mouth, and then they put me into a large sack. . . . The next day proved a day of greater sorrow than I had yet experienced; for my sister and I were then separated, while we lay clasped in each other's arms. It was in vain that we besought them not to part us; she was torn from me, and immediately carried away. . . ."

—Olaudah Equiano, an African born to a noble family, taken into slavery when he was just a boy

After eleven years as a slave, Equiano was freed. Around 1756, he published a best-selling autobiography in hopes that his description of the evils of slavery would help end the awful institution.

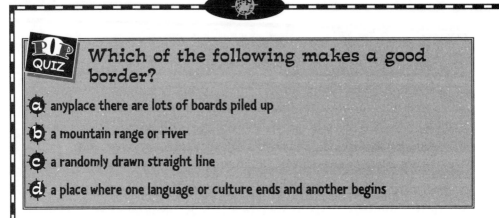

POP QUIZ

Which of the following makes a good border?

a anyplace there are lots of boards piled up

b a mountain range or river

c a randomly drawn straight line

d a place where one language or culture ends and another begins

Letters "b" and "d" are almost always preferable to letters "a" and "c." Natural boundaries are just that—more natural. When people draw borders for other reasons, they can cause long-term problems.

Picture this: One day, a stranger comes along and draws a line down the middle of your street. Then he tells you, in a foreign language, that tomorrow you have to go to a new school and obey a king who lives very far away. You can no longer get your groceries across the street because that's now another country, and there isn't another store for miles around. Worse yet, your best friend also lives across the street and can no longer come over and play. But lucky you, the bully on your block is in your country, and it's either get along with him or go to war.

That's just about what happened in Africa in the 1880s. Europeans began to explore the inside of the continent, and soon they were as hungry for African land as they'd been for African people. Many European nations, primarily Britain, France, Germany, Italy, Portugal, and Belgium, came in and divvied up the continent among themselves, saying the Africans would benefit from education and the Christian religion. Not a thought was given to what Africans wanted or where traditional tribal boundaries were. Africa became a continent of colonies, or lands ruled by foreign countries.

Why is it hard to remember the names of the countries in Africa?

Not only because there are so many, but also because the names keep changing. By 1991, all the African colonies had gained their independence from their European rulers. Many changed their European-given names as symbols of their freedom. The Belgian Congo became Zaire, and then the Democratic Republic of the Congo. French Somaliland became Djibouti. Rhodesia became Zimbabwe, and so forth.

WELCOME TO
~~BELGIAN CONGO~~
~~ZAIRE~~
DEMOCRATIC REPUBLIC OF THE CONGO

Africa's first independent country was Liberia, whose name comes from the Latin word for "free." Liberia was started as a colony for freed American slaves.

POP QUIZ

Which one of these is the capital of South Africa?

a Pretoria

c Bloemfontein

b Cape Town

d all of the above

The answer is "d." South Africa has not one, not two, but three capitals. Pretoria is the administrative capital, where the business of governing takes place. Cape Town is the legislative capital, where laws are made. Bloemfontein is the judicial capital, home of the independent courts.

What sound does the Horn of Africa make?

Since the Horn isn't a musical instrument but a point of land on the eastern side of the continent, it doesn't make any sound at all. But if you could hear it, you'd probably hear the sounds of war. The area, which looks like the horn of a rhinoceros jutting out into the Indian Ocean, includes the countries Ethiopia, Eritrea, Djibouti, and Somalia. In the past few decades, these countries have fought costly civil wars among their many clans and tribes. In addition to deaths from violence, many people have died of hunger and malnourishment. Food is scarce because of drought and poor farming methods, and the fighting in the Horn, as in other parts of Africa, uses up money and resources that would otherwise be spent on growing and transporting crops.

Is Africa crowded?

People who hear about population problems in African countries sometimes think that the continent is densely populated. In fact, people are spread very unevenly across Africa, and most of the land has few inhabitants. In sub-Saharan Africa especially, more than 70 percent of the people are scattered thinly across the land as farmers, trying to make a living with soil that is often too dry, too wet, or too disease ridden to support them well. Others have crowded into a few densely packed cities, such as Lagos in Nigeria, or Kinshasa in the Democratic Republic of the Congo.

The problem is that, even in farm areas, the population has gone beyond the land's carrying capacity, or the greatest number of people that a region can sustain with its food and water. Despite this, populations are booming in many countries. The population of most sub-Saharan countries will double in twenty to thirty years. (In the United States, the population won't double for another hundred years.) Africa also has more refugees—people driven from their homes by war or famine—than any other continent. Africans hope that a new generation of African-born leaders will lead them into a brighter future.

As the millennium began, one of the most pressing issues facing Africa was the fatal disease AIDS. By the time 1999 had ended, 84 percent of the world's 16.3 million AIDS deaths had occurred in sub-Saharan Africa. In some countries, more than one out of every five people was infected with HIV, the virus that causes AIDS. Because of the rapid spread of this disease, the average life expectancy in sub-Saharan Africa is expected to fall from fifty-nine years to forty-five years by the year 2010. African nations are now doing more to educate their citizens about the disease's causes and prevention—and hoping for a cure.

CHAPTER 5

ASIA

WHAT'S SO GREAT ABOUT THE GREAT WALL OF CHINA?

BIGGEST, HIGHEST, DEEPEST...

SIZE: Largest continent: 17,213,298 sq mi (44,579,000 sq km)

HIGHEST MOUNTAIN: Everest: 29,035 ft (8,850 m)

LOWEST POINT: Shores of the Dead Sea: 1,339 ft (408 m) below sea level

LARGEST LAKE: Caspian Sea: 143,244 sq mi (371,000 sq km)

LONGEST RIVER: Chang (Yangtze): 3,964 mi (6,380 km)

LARGEST DESERT: Gobi: 500,000 sq mi (1,294,994 sq km)

LARGEST ISLAND: Borneo: 280,137 sq mi (725,500 sq km)

How is Asia like a state fair?

Like state fairs that boast exhibits such as "World's Tallest Man!" and "Largest Pumpkin Ever Grown!", Asia has a lot of things that are "biggest" or "most" in the world. It is the world's biggest continent and home to most of the world's people (3,637,000,000, or 6 out of every 10 Earth dwellers). It has the world's biggest country (Russia: 6,592,692 square miles, or 17,075,000 sq km*) and two most populous countries (China, with 1,254,062,000 people, and India, with 1,002,142,000). It also has the highest point on Earth (Mount Everest), the lowest point on Earth (the Dead Sea), and biggest lake on Earth (the Caspian Sea).

* About a third of Russia is actually in Europe, but most of it is in Asia. As you saw with lakes called seas, geography is an inexact science.

What world language has the most speakers?

You might think it's English, but it's actually Mandarin Chinese (which makes sense when you know that China has more people than any other country). Hindi comes in second, followed by Spanish, English, Bengali, and Arabic. There are more than 200 languages in the world that have at least one million speakers.

POP QUIZ

If you're on the "roof of the world," where are you?

ⓐ dangling from clouds

ⓑ on the top floor of one of Malaysia's Petronas Towers, the tallest buildings on Earth

ⓒ near the Himalaya mountains

The answer is letter "c." The Himalayas are the highest group, or range, of mountains in the world (measuring from sea level). Behind the Himalayas, you'll find China's Tibetan plateau, an area of high, flat land. The average height of this plateau is 15,000 feet (4,500 m) high, making it the highest region on Earth, so it's known as the "roof of the world."

TRUE OR FALSE The Himalaya Mountains grow taller every year.

True! Not only are the Himalayas the tallest mountains on the planet, they're getting taller every year. That's because of the way they were made. Think back to continental drift and plate tectonics from Chapter 1. The plate carrying India plowed into and under the plate carrying Asia about

40 to 60 million years ago, and where they met, the land on top folded up like an accordion. The pressure of one plate pushing under the other is still enough to lift up the mountains roughly a centimeter, or about the length of your pinky nail, each year.

What song could people in southern Asia sing all summer?

"It's raining, it's pouring . . ." All summer long, heavy rains accompany the monsoon winds that blow in from the ocean. Monsoons are winds that change directions with the seasons. When the winds blow from land to sea in winter, they're dry. But when they blow from sea to land in summer, they're warm and wet. They carry lots and lots of rain with them.

Is all that rain good or bad? It depends. Many people in southern Asia (and also in central Africa and northern Australia) are farmers who have built their lives around the heavy rains of monsoon season. Rice growers in Southeast Asia, especially, welcome the warm, rainy weather needed for their crops to grow. But the rains aren't always good. If they come too late or not at all, there will be little or nothing to eat. And if too much rain falls, floods will destroy crops and villages.

Why does one side of the Himalaya range hog all the monsoon rains?

The Himalayas are very, very tall. They're like a big wall across south Asia. And like many other mountain ranges, they're wet on one side and mostly dry on the other.

Tall mountaintops keep clouds from getting from one side to the other. When winds blow in from the ocean, they carry lots of moisture with them. And when the wind meets the mountains, the air is forced to rise, cool, and form clouds. Because the mountains are in the way, the clouds drop nearly all their rain on the windward side, leaving the opposite, leeward side dry. The windward side of the Himalayas gets 200 to 600 inches (500 to 1,500 cm) of rain a year, while the leeward side usually gets less than 10 inches (25 cm).

Who invented cities?

Cities weren't really "invented." They just happened out of necessity. But if you had to say who the first urban planners were, it would probably be the ancient Mesopotamians and Egyptians. The first humans were hunter-gatherers who were always on the move in search of food. But when farming began about 10,000 years ago, things began to change. Farms could support more people per acre of land than hunting or gathering. Some people could stop producing their own food and concentrate on other specialties. Domesticated animals could help carry the food to centers of population.

The world's first civilizations arose in fertile river valleys in Asia, including the valleys of the Huang (Yellow) River in China, the Tigris and Euphrates Rivers in the Middle East, and the Nile in Egypt. The first real cities were also in Asia. They were the capitals of the ancient empires that thrived around the Mediterranean Sea and in the Middle East. Possibly the world's first great empire was Sumer, founded 5,000 to 6,000 years ago in Mesopotamia, the area between the Tigris and Euphrates Rivers in present-day Iraq. Its capital, Ur, was founded about the same time as the Egyptian capitals of Thebes and Memphis.

Which of the following were developed or invented in Asia?

Astronomy, domestication of animals, cultivation of wheat, the wheel, clay pottery, iron and steel tools, Western religions (Christianity, Islam, Judaism), alphabets, cities, the bow and arrow, calendars, writing, zeros, sewers, bricks, charcoal, maps, spun wool, glass, steam power, kites, calculators, compasses, beer.

All of 'em!

What's so great about the Great Wall of China?

The Great Wall of China is the largest artificial structure on Earth: it's almost 3,000 miles (4,828 km) long! (It covers 1,500 miles (2,414 km) of ground, but with all its snaking around, the wall is almost twice that long. If you walked 2½ miles an hour all day and all night, it would take you more than seven weeks to get from one end of the wall to the other.

The wall was built to protect China from Mongol warrior tribes who lived to the north. (Good thing the Himalayas formed a natural wall to the south so the Chinese didn't need to worry about invaders from that direction.) The Great Wall was started around 221 B.C. by the first emperor of China, Shihuangdi. Building the first section of the wall was such exhausting and dangerous work that it killed tens of thousands of workers. It's said that their bodies were just tossed into the dirt to become part of the earthen wall.

Over the next 2,000 years or so, many rulers added sections and watchtowers to the wall, which averages 25 feet (7.6 m) in height and 12 feet (3.66 m) in thickness. The wall is intimidating by itself, but watchmen and warriors were necessary to really make the defense effective. The Mongols outsmarted the defenders along the wall twice. In the early thirteenth century, they broke through the wall, and in 1644, they went around it. Both times, they took over China.

Was the Silk Road made of fine, delicate fabric?

It was anything but delicate. Opened around 110 B.C., what became known as the Silk Road was one of history's oldest, longest, roughest, and most important trade routes. It crossed 4,000 miles (6,400 km) of Asia's rugged mountains and scorching deserts to connect the Mediterranean in the West with China in the East. The extraordinary route carried silk, gems, spices, skills, knowledge, ideas, and religions between the empires that ruled the opposite ends of Asia.

What kind of stories did Marco Polo tell?

Wild ones, as far as Europeans were concerned. Marco Polo was the son of a Venetian merchant and one of the best-known early travelers to China. Even after the Silk Road had been open for more than a thousand years, the East was mysterious to Europeans. Few had traveled all the way to "Cathay," as they called China. Instead, merchants sent their goods through a network of traders that extended from Europe to China. But around 1245, that began to change. A tribe of warriors called the Mongols conquered nearly all the lands between East and West, making travel between the two easier.

Though it wasn't as valuable as rubies or emeralds, one of the tastier items Marco Polo found in the East was ice cream. The frozen dessert probably began as the flavored ice served in ancient Rome. But after the Roman Empire fell, ice cream disappeared from Europe until Marco Polo brought recipes from the East. Polo's recipe was more like today's, with milk as the main ingredient.

Marco Polo was just a teenager in 1271, when he and his father and uncle made the three-and-a-half-year trek across Asia. Young Polo spent seventeen years touring Asia in the service of the Chinese emperor, Kublai Khan, then returned to Europe with rubies, emeralds, diamonds, and plenty of tales of all the riches and splendor he'd seen. His accounts of palaces decorated with gold and silver, fireworks made from gunpowder, printed books, and paper money were so incredible to Europeans that many thought he must have made them up.

"In this city Kublai Khan built a huge palace of marble and other ornamental stones. Its halls and chambers are all gilded, and the whole building is marvelously embellished and richly adorned.... In the midst of this enclosed park, where there is a beautiful grove, the Great Khan has built another large palace, constructed entirely of canes, but with the interior all gilt and decorated with beasts and birds of very skillful workmanship....The roof is also made of canes, so well varnished that it is quite waterproof.... And the Great Khan has had it so designed that it can be moved whenever he fancies; for it is held in place by more than two hundred cords of silk."

—From Marco Polo's *Travels of Marco Polo*, describing Kublai Khan's park in Shang-tu, or Beijing, around 1275

Why didn't Arab or Asian sailors find the Americas?

Basically because they weren't out looking for trade routes, the way Europeans were. By the Middle Ages, the Arabs had already established trade with the East. And though they didn't mind spreading their religion, Islam, the Arabs didn't feel compelled to do it the way Christian Europeans did.

The Chinese weren't looking for trading partners because they felt they already had everything they needed. They also weren't especially fond of strangers. (Thus the Great Wall, to keep them out.) So though the Chinese had been some of the greatest early shipbuilders and the inventors of the compass, after sailing the South Seas to India, East Africa, and Indonesia, they turned inward.

What is the Middle East in the middle of?

The middle of the East—sort of. The "East," or Asia, is so big that Europeans once broke it up into the Near East (eastern Europe, western Asia, and northern Africa), the Far East (Southeast Asia, China, Japan, and Korea), and the Middle East (everything in between). Today, the Middle East usually means Israel, Egypt, and the Arabian Peninsula (Saudi Arabia and surrounding countries).

In ancient times, the Middle East was the middle of the known world. The area is the crossroads of three continents: Asia, Europe, and Africa. Anyone trading from East to West had to stop there, which is what helped make the area's ancient empires—Egypt, Babylonia, Rome, Greece, the Arab and Ottoman empires—so great.

PIP QUIZ

The city of Jerusalem, in Israel, is holy to people of which religion(s):

a Judaism

d Hinduism

b Islam

e Buddhism

c Christianity

The answers are "a," "b," and "c." These three major world religions started in the Middle East thousands of years ago. (The world's other major religions, Hinduism and Buddhism, also started in Asia, in India.) The three Middle Eastern religions all have some connection to Jerusalem. To Jews, the city is the ancient capital of Israel; to Christians, it's the site of the crucifixion, burial, and resurrection of Jesus; and to Muslims, it's the place where Mohammed ascended to Heaven. Today, all three religions continue to struggle for a hold on the city that is sacred to all of them.

What is the blackest, slimiest, gooiest treasure on Earth?

Oil. Oil is a valuable, nonrenewable resource. It is used in fabric, carpets, detergents, makeup, aspirin, plastics, and toothpaste, and is also used as fuel to run our cars and boats and planes and to heat our homes and buildings. Half of the power produced in the world comes from oil.

The deserts of the Arabian Peninsula sit on top of about a third of the world's known oil reserves, which gives the area a lot of global power. The discovery of oil there in the 1930s changed a poor land of shepherds and tents into a rich land of businesspeople and office buildings. But even with all that wealth and oil, the land of sand is without something that may be even more valuable: water. In the deserts of the Arabian Peninsula, there's not a river in sight.

If Russia is so big, why doesn't it have more people?

Because so much of the country has a cold and distinctly unfriendly climate. The northern region known as Siberia occupies more than half of Russia but has less than 20 percent of its population because of frigid temperatures, permanently frozen soil, and winters where the Sun never really rises. Siberia is the coldest place on the planet besides Antarctica. It's so desolate that it became a place where Russian leaders sent prisoners as punishment. The native people who live in Siberia herd reindeer and trap furs. But not many people choose to live there year-round.

To the south of the coldest part of Siberia are evergreen forests called taiga. But few people live even there. To find most Russians, you have to go south and west to the steppes, the grassy, treeless plains, and to Russia's big cities, such as Moscow and St. Petersburg.

Why can't we get at most of Siberia's natural resources?

Although Siberia is rich in coal, oil, and other minerals, it's hard to get those resources out of the permafrost, or permanently frozen ground. One of Siberia's more accessible, and much more beautiful, resources is enormous Lake Baikal, the deepest lake in the world. Lake Baikal and its surroundings are home to almost 1,500 species of animals found nowhere else in the world. The lake was clean and peaceful until businesses began cutting down trees and dumping industrial wastes into the once crystal-clear lake water. Teams of Russian and international scientists are now trying to save the ancient lake.

WHAT WAS THE "THIRD WORLD"?

It sounds like something out of science fiction, but really it was much less glamorous. The term "Third World" was first used in the 1950s to describe countries in Asia, Africa, and South America that were poor or underdeveloped. At that time, the world's two superpowers were the United States and the Soviet Union (U.S.S.R.). The "First World" was the United States and its allies; the "Second World" was the Soviet Union and its allies; the "Third World" was everyone left over. When the Soviet Union fell apart in 1991, the distinctions made no sense. Though today we might talk about "developed" and "developing" countries, most people try not to use terms that make one part of the world sound superior to another.

If you lived in India, would your parents arrange your marriage?

Quite possibly, if you were a member of the Hindu religion. About 80 percent of Indians practice Hinduism, the oldest major religion in the world. Hinduism began in India, and most of its followers still live there. Hindus worship many gods and believe in reincarnation, or the rebirth of a person's soul during many lives. Another important aspect of traditional Hindu life is the caste system, which separates followers into four social classes: priests and scholars; warriors, rulers, and landowners; farmers, traders, and merchants; and laborers, artisans, and servants. Below the castes are the "untouchables." Members of different castes are not supposed to associate with one another, so jobs and marriage are restricted. The only way to a higher caste is by reincarnation in the next life.

Many groups and individuals have challenged the rigid caste system. The system broke down a bit while the British ruled India (1858–1947) and as a result of the nonviolent protests of a Hindu leader named Mohandas Gandhi. Today the caste system is still very much alive, though it's become more flexible in cities where members of different castes mingle more often. Practicing untouchability and discrimination based on caste are now illegal.

What is India's official language?

Assamese, Bengali, Gujarati, Hindi, Kannada, Kashmiri, Malayalam, Marathi, Oriya, Punjabi, Sanskrit, Sindi, Tamil, Telugu, and Urdu. Yes, India has fifteen official languages, due to the great variety of ethnic groups who live there. Beginning with the Aryans, who invaded southern Asia about 6,000 years ago, many different peoples have moved into India and settled down in various regions of the big country, bringing their languages with them. Hindi is spoken or understood by about half the country. In addition, many people speak English as a common second language, a practice dating from the days when India was ruled by the British.

What saying could be Japan's national motto?

"When life hands you lemons, make lemonade." (In other words, when you get something sour, use it to make something sweet.)

Japan is one of the world's great success stories. It's one of the wealthiest and most productive nations, yet geographically speaking, it got all lemons. Japan is built on a mountainous string of islands on the Ring of Fire in the Pacific Ocean. It's surrounded by forty active volcanoes and can have as many as fifteen significant earthquakes a year. It has barely a drop of oil, and only 15 percent of its land is farmable. Yet it has lots and lots of people to feed.

The strengths Japan does have are citizens with lots of ideas, energy, skill, and education who work toward common goals. As an island people, the Japanese eat mostly fish they catch and rice they can produce themselves. They invest money in business and technology. And in a culture that prizes hard work, they focus on making the best products possible. In the 1990s, Japan was number one or two in the world in making VCRs, TVs, microwaves, computers, copy machines, refrigerators, watches, and cameras.

Looking for Japan on a map of the Pacific? The four main islands and more than a thousand small islets that form its archipelago look something like a dragon.

What do you get when you add 13,000 islands together?

A country: Indonesia, to be exact. Several Southeast Asian countries are on archipelagos, large groups or chains of islands. Indonesia stretches across more than 13,000 islands; the country of the Philippines is also made of thousands of islands. Sailors following the monsoon winds that blow through these tropical nations brought in many different Asian religions, traditions, and goods, such as cloth and mangoes.

POP QUIZ: Where is the world's tallest building?

a. Tokyo, Japan

c. New York, New York

b. Chicago, Illinois

d. Kuala Lumpur, Malaysia

The answer is "d." The World Trade Center in New York City was the world's tallest building until the Sears Tower was built in Chicago, and the Sears Tower was the tallest until Malaysia's Petronas Towers were finished in 1998. Malaysia's Towers are an example of how many small island nations in Asia's Pacific Rim have gone from being developing nations to being modern economic powerhouses in a short time. Countries like South Korea, Taiwan, and Singapore have few natural resources, so, like Japan, they concentrate on the manufacturing and shipping of goods. All these places are at least three-quarters, if not entirely, urban, and they have excellent deep-water ports that can take large ships.

Why do so many things in America say "Made in Taiwan"?

Because nearly 40 percent of what the United States imports is made in China, Taiwan, or another Pacific Rim country. Goods made there are less expensive than those produced in the United States, because skilled workers in those countries are paid less money. People disagree about whether this is good or bad. Some say that, even though we can get products for less, the practice takes jobs away from Americans. Others say that the average American benefits from getting cheaper goods. Both sides note that these jobs often involve long hours and poor conditions, making life hard for the workers.

CHAPTER 6

EUROPE

IS "EURO" A NICKNAME FOR EUROPEANS?

BIGGEST, HIGHEST, DEEPEST . . .

Size

Sixth-largest continent: 4,066,241 sq mi (10,530,750 sq km)

Highest mountain

El'brus: 18,510 ft (5,642 m)

Lowest point

Caspian Sea (European side): 92 ft (28 m) below sea level

Largest lake

Ladoga: 6,853 sq mi (17,703 sq km)

Largest island

Great Britain: 84,215 sq mi (218,100 sq km)

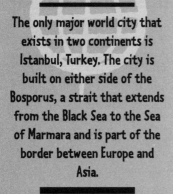

The only major world city that exists in two continents is Istanbul, Turkey. The city is built on either side of the Bosporus, a strait that extends from the Black Sea to the Sea of Marmara and is part of the border between Europe and Asia.

Where does Europe end and Asia begin?

If you look at a map of the world, you'll see that Europe is a huge peninsula, an area of land surrounded on three sides by water, that sticks out of one side of Asia's landmass. Yet the culture, religion, history, politics, and languages of Europe are quite different from those of Asia. So geographers divide the landmass into two continents along the Ural Mountains and the Caspian and Black Seas. (Russia and Turkey straddle that line, just to be difficult.)

The answer is "b." Almost every part of Europe is within a few hundred miles of an ocean or a big bay. That means three things: One, Europe has lots of beaches. Two, the continent has pretty mild weather most of the year, because ocean currents keep the land from getting very hot or very cold. And three, throughout recorded history its people have taken to the sea as traders, explorers, and even pirates.

The peninsula that is Europe has lots of smaller peninsulas all along its coastline. One of the most recognizable is Italy. You can find it on a map because it looks like a boot.

The Europeans who went gallivanting to various parts of the globe—Marco Polo to China, Vasco da Gama to India, Christopher Columbus and the Spanish conquistadors to the Americas, James Cook to Australia and nearly Antarctica—spread Western, or European, culture around the world. On the heels of the explorers came merchants and missionaries, who spread European goods and religion. And on the heels of the merchants and missionaries came settlers, who set up colonies in many far-flung places.

Was there a Troy?

Yes—lots of them, all built on top of each other. The ancient city of Troy, in what is now western Turkey, was the site of the legendary Greek and Trojan War that the Greek poet Homer told of in the *Iliad*, more than 2,000 years ago. After ten years of fighting, the story goes, the Greeks finally won the war by building, and hiding in, a huge wooden horse outside the walls of Troy. When the intrigued Trojans wheeled the horse into the city, the Greeks climbed out, let in the rest of their army, and burned the city to the ground.

No one knew whether ancient Troy really existed until its ruins were found by a curious German named Heinrich Schliemann more than a hundred years ago. Eight levels of Troy were uncovered, with newer ones built on top of older ones.

What disease did Europeans get in the fifteenth century?

They got a bad case of Exploration Fever. Marco Polo's tales made Europeans hungrier than ever for the riches of India, China, and the "Spice Islands" of the East. They knew that whoever dominated the trade for those silks, spices, and precious stones would become rich and powerful. But rather than stumble through foreign mountains and deserts as Marco Polo had done, they began to search for a sea route to the East.

Spices were in high demand in Europe because they originally grew only in south Asia. Though most people think spices were used to flavor and preserve food, they were valued primarily for their use in making medicines.

The idea was to go around Africa. Problem was, no one knew how big Africa was. How far south did it go? Was there a way around it at all? The Greeks had proposed nearly 2,000 years before that a great continent must exist in the far south to balance out all the land in the north. Was Africa connected to this unknown southern land? More important to most sailors, would the waters around Africa boil and be filled with man-eating serpents?

One young European thought these stories were rubbish. Portugal's Prince Henry the Navigator, intensely curious but not a sailor himself, sent more than fifteen expeditions of fearful sailors down the western coast of Africa into the Great Unknown. Henry's sailors didn't get far before their patron died in 1460, but neither did they encounter any menacing monsters or sizzling waters. Henry's men paved the way for other Portuguese sailors. In 1487, Bartholomeu Dias rounded the southern tip of Africa. Ten years later, Vasco da Gama sailed around the tip and continued north to India.

How are England, Great Britain, and the United Kingdom different?

Here's how: England is a country. It is located on an island called Great Britain, which it shares with the countries of Scotland and Wales. Those three countries join with a fourth—Northern Ireland, on an island just west of Great Britain—to form one political unit called the United Kingdom. The people of the three countries on Great Britain are often referred to, as a group, as the British.

Is there one Ireland, or two?

Two. Northern Ireland, which occupies the northeast corner of the island of Ireland, is part of the United Kingdom. The rest of the island is an independent country known as the Republic of Ireland.

All of Ireland used to be a single country and a colony of England. In 1920, it split in two. The Republic of Ireland gained its independence, but Northern Ireland, where many English and Scottish people had settled, remained under English control. Both countries have suffered from religious conflicts between Catholics (the majority in the Republic) and Protestants (the majority in Northern Ireland). Many Irish in the north also don't like being ruled by the British. The political and religious conflict, often called Ireland's "Troubles," has caused lots of violence and many terrorist attacks in Ireland and Great Britain.

Are there emeralds in the Emerald Isle?

Nope. Ireland got its nickname because its countryside is so green. Like the other British Isles, Ireland stays relatively mild and gets lots of rain because of the warm ocean currents that flow around Ireland and Great Britain.

Why do people in so many different parts of the world speak English?

Because they were all once ruled by the people of a small European island that was the birthplace of Shakespeare, Prince Charles, the Loch Ness Monster, and Alice in Wonderland. Which one? You've probably guessed it—it's Great Britain. The island of Great Britain is just a little more than half the size of California. Yet the British people created an empire that, at its height in the 1880s and 1890s, ruled one-quarter of the world's land and one-fifth of its people. The saying "the sun never sets on the British Empire" was entirely true.

Geography has a lot to do with Great Britain's success. Surrounded by water, the island withstood invasions for 900 years. The famous white cliffs of Dover

Great Britain isn't as isolated as it once was. In 1994, the Chunnel (short for Channel Tunnel, a tunnel under the English Channel) connected Great Britain with mainland Europe for the first time since the Ice Age. Now British and French travelers who used to have to take airplanes or ferry boats across the Channel can take a speedy thirty-five-minute train ride to visit—or just have lunch with—their neighbors.

face invaders from mainland Europe, providing extra armor. And because the roads to any other nation were paved with water, Great Britain naturally developed a strong navy that came to rule the seas. That navy sailed around the world collecting colonies, from which the British took resources that helped them become even more rich and powerful.

Why are there so many resorts in the Alps?

The Alps are Europe's most famous mountain chain, and no wonder: they boast spectacular, snow-capped peaks and glacial lakes, lots of easily traveled roads, and plenty of outdoor sports. For the devoted mountain climber there are Mont Blanc, Europe's second-highest peak, and the Matterhorn, whose steep, sheer sides have challenged many a mountaineer.

The Alps have a number of natural valleys and mountain passes, so they don't separate people the way the Himalayas do. (But they don't exactly make it easy to bond, either.) The Alps form a natural boundary between the Germanic culture and cool climate to the north and the Mediterranean cultures and warmer climate to the south.

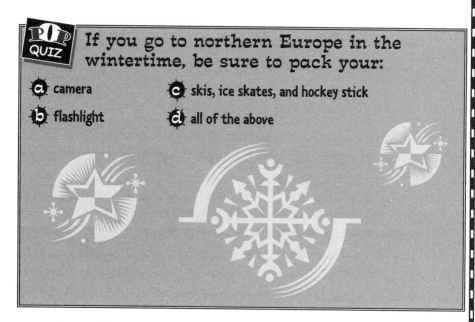

POP QUIZ

If you go to northern Europe in the wintertime, be sure to pack your:

a camera

b flashlight

c skis, ice skates, and hockey stick

d all of the above

The answer is "d." The chilly Nordic countries of Sweden, Norway, Denmark, Finland, and Iceland, commonly known as Scandinavia, are another European haven of winter sports. (Except for Denmark, flat and marshy. That's a good place to go bicycling.) When you've put away your sporting equipment, you'll want your camera to take pictures of the area's majestic scenery. Scandinavia has rugged mountains, vast evergreen forests, and stunning fjords. Fjords are the jagged ocean inlets around Norway's coast that were formed by rivers and glaciers. (There are fjords in North and South America and New Zealand, but Norway's are the most famous.) The fjords are not only breathtaking, but useful. Rivers and waterfalls that pour down from the mountains provide a huge amount of hydroelectric power.

But winter in Scandinavia isn't all scenery and skiing. The region has long been called the Land of the Midnight Sun because, in its northern regions, the Sun doesn't set for at least one night each summer. (Remember that Earth is tilted, and Scandinavia is close to the North Pole.) It's the opposite during the dead of winter. You'll want your flashlight, because the Sun rarely rises above the horizon. Even in southern Scandinavia, winter days can be short and gloomy.

How icy is Iceland?

Not very. Like Greenland, Iceland doesn't really live up to its name. The winters in Iceland's capital, Reykjavik, aren't much worse than those in New York City. Vikings who spent two harsh winters there in the 800s named the island, but the harshness comes more from the area's rugged land than from its weather. About 80 percent of Iceland consists of mountains, rocky plateaus, and snow fields. But Iceland's weather is usually mild because it's warmed by an ocean current called the North Atlantic Drift Current and by the many hot springs it has underground. These hot springs also light up the island: 80 percent of the country's power comes from geothermal energy.

What has western Europe exported to the world?

Knowledge, music, literature, and art. Western Europe has produced more than its fair share of these ever since the Greeks made major achievements in the arts, architecture, science, math, philosophy,

literature, and democracy nearly 2,500 years ago. The Romans soaked up the Greeks' accomplishments and added to them, dominating the Mediterranean for almost 1,000 years. More recently, Europe has produced the likes of Shakespeare, Mozart, Tchaikovsky, Beethoven, Michelangelo, Picasso, Newton, Einstein, Dickens, and countless others. (Not to mention French wine and fashion, Swiss watches, German chocolate cake, French toast, Polish sausage, and Swedish meatballs!) Today, this part of Europe is still home to many of the world's great centers of culture: London, Paris, Rome, Berlin. No wonder there are so many tourists in Europe! If they're not playing sports in the Alps, they're absorbing culture in the cities.

Why are there so many cities in Europe?

Most cities are born as defensive forts, or as crossroads of trade and transportation routes along rivers, such as Europe's many accessible waterways. Once there are a lot of people living in the same area, the place attracts services and cultural institutions. The services attract even more people, and the city grows. Then more services come to help the new people, and—well, you get the point. This is the way many of Europe's metropolises grew. Huge cities such as Moscow, London, Paris, and Madrid are now connected to many smaller, busy urban areas by rail, road, and river. Today the world's second-smallest continent is also the second-most populated, so it's very crowded.

Is Benelux a kind of automobile?

Nah. Belgium, the Netherlands, and Luxembourg are three small but prosperous countries that are sometimes called by the collective name of Benelux. Located close to the North Sea and Great Britain, these countries have benefited from easy access to world trade through their harbors. Belgium and the Netherlands used to rule colonies around the world, becoming rich from trading foreign goods such as spices, woods, and chocolate. (Even today, Belgian chocolates are some of the best in the world.)

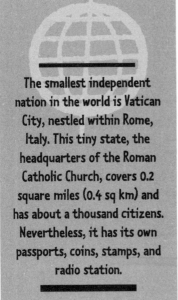

Belgium, the Netherlands, and Luxembourg are also sometimes called the Low Countries. This isn't meant to be insulting. It just means that the land is literally very low. Almost half of the Netherlands is below sea level. Making the best of a soggy situation, the country has drained and pumped dry quite a bit of land, reclaiming it from the sea.

Where in Europe do you take a boat to the grocery store?

In Venice, Italy. Venice is a coastal city built on more than a hundred tiny islands connected by hundreds of bridges. Instead of highways, the city has waterways, called canals. Venice was born as a marketplace because it was easy for ships to get in and out of the city. By the Middle Ages, it had become rich trading in silk and spices from the East.

How does Europe keep mapmakers hopping?

It keeps making, breaking, and remaking countries. Mapmakers had to redraw boundaries over and over again in the twentieth century as two world wars and the disappearance of the Soviet Union changed political ties in Europe.

Before World War I, a handful of large nations such as the German Empire and the Austro-Hungarian Empire controlled much of Europe. The war broke up and remade many of those countries; Poland, Czechoslovakia, Hungary, and others appeared. World War II split Germany into two parts, which were rejoined in 1989. Meanwhile, the Soviet Union, a group of fifteen republics formed  by Russia after World War I, split apart into republics again by 1991. Cartographers were grateful that they had computers by then: at least they didn't have to redraw these maps by hand.

Is changing a country's boundaries as easy as redrawing lines on a map?

For mapmakers it might be, but not for the people living within or around those lines. When the Soviet Union fell apart, national conflicts that had been controlled by the tight Soviet rule were unleashed. People of eastern Europe's many different ethnic groups (meaning they have a particular religion, race, culture, or nation) began fighting over whose land was whose.

This was especially true in the former country of Yugoslavia. Yugoslavia was haphazardly created when the Austro-Hungarian Empire broke up after World War I. Bad idea. Many separate ethnic groups had developed in the area's isolated valleys, and with different cultures, the groups had never been friends. After the Soviet government vanished, cruel, bloody wars broke out in Yugoslavia. Today the country has split into five independent nations, but more fighting can ignite at any time.

Is there a Transylvania?

Yes! The home of the fanged namesake of Bram Stoker's novel, *Dracula*, is a region in central Romania. The vampire character of Count Dracula was based on a real person, the medieval Prince Vlad III, who was known for his atrocious murders. Prince Vlad's castle still stands in Transylvania.

Is "Euro" a nickname for Europeans?

No. The Euro is the common currency of the countries that have formed the European Union, or EU. Fifteen countries—France, Germany, the United Kingdom, the Netherlands, Belgium, Luxembourg, Austria, Italy, Ireland, Denmark, Sweden, Finland, Portugal, Spain, and Greece—make up the union, which was created in 1993 to help the countries become a stronger economic force. In 1999, the EU created its new currency for all the countries to use. The Euro will be in full circulation by 2002. It may give the economy a boost, but many people will miss their distinctive French francs, German marks, and Italian lira.

CHAPTER 7

NORTH AMERICA

WHY ISN'T AMERICA CALLED COLUMBIA?

BIGGEST, HIGHEST, DEEPEST . . .

Size

Third-largest continent:
9,366,000 sq mi (24,256,000
sq km)

Highest mountain

McKinley (Denali): 20,320 ft
(6,194 m)

Lowest point

Death Valley: 282 ft (86 m)
below sea level

Largest lake

Lake Superior: 31,701 sq mi
(82,100 sq km)

Longest river

Mississippi-Missouri: 3,710 mi
(5,971 km)

Largest island

Greenland: 840,004 sq mi
(2,175,600 sq km)

What gets smaller as you go north in North America?

The population. Not too many people live in northern North America, which is closer to the North Pole than land in any other continent. The huge North American island of Greenland, which is a province of Denmark, has about 58,000 people, fewer than some large towns in the United States. Canada is the second-largest country in the world, but, like Russia, much of its land is cold, barren tundra (treeless Arctic plains). Eighty percent of Canadians live in the south, within 100 miles of the Canada–United States border. Most people in the United States live on its coasts and in the midwestern states that are major suppliers of wheat, corn, soybeans, and beef to the rest of the world.

Does North America stop at the south Texas border?

Hardly, pardner. Most geographers say that North America consists of twenty-three countries, from Canada and the United States to Mexico, the countries of Central America down through Panama, and the islands of the Caribbean.

What colossal canyon did the Colorado River carve?

Like a slow but powerful drill, the river carved the Grand Canyon in the southwestern United States. A canyon is usually a long narrow valley that rises steeply on both sides. The Grand Canyon is long—277 miles (446 km)—and a mile deep in places, but it's far from narrow. It ranges from 1 to 18 miles (1.6 to 29 km) wide! The breathtaking canyon is even more amazing when you consider that all that space was once filled with rock. Little by little, over millions of years, the raging Colorado has worn away the rock in the high Colorado plateau. Since the erosion process started so long ago, you have the feeling of walking through time when you walk down into the canyon—the layers of rock get older as you go down. Many of the exposed layers of rock contain fossils, or remains of plants and animals that lived up to 560 million years ago.

Where did *The Wizard of Oz* take place?

In Kansas, right in the middle of America's "tornado alley." Nine out of ten tornadoes, the kind of wind funnel that swept Dorothy and Toto off to Oz, happen in the United States. And though they can happen anywhere in the country, they most often hit the states right in the country's flat midsection, from Texas to Iowa. Here, cold, dry air from Canada meets warm, wet air from the Gulf of Mexico, breeding intense thunderstorms and their violent children, tornadoes. The National Weather Service says about seventy people are killed by the 800 or so tornadoes that hit the United States each year.

Where did the word "hurricane" come from?

From the Caribbean, and for a good reason: The Caribbean Sea gets hit with more hurricanes than any other region in the Atlantic. "Hurakan" was originally the name of a Mayan god of the sky. Natives of the

Caribbean picked up the name to use for the violent storms that came at them from the air.

On average, five hurricanes sweep through the Caribbean every year. Fifteen of the twenty most dangerous Atlantic hurricanes in history have hit the islands and Central America. They include Hurricane Mitch, which blasted the country of Honduras in 1998, killing more than 9,000 people; Flora, which killed about 8,000 in Haiti and Cuba in 1962; and an unnamed monster in 1930 that killed about 8,000 in the Dominican Republic.

Why are most of North America's lakes in the northern part of the continent?

To find the answer, we'll have to go back in time. Grab your warmest coat, because we're going back about 15,000 years to the last ice age. North America looked awfully different back then. More than half the continent was covered with huge sheets of ice and snow called glaciers. The glaciers formed in Canada and slid their way down the continent. As they crept along, the glaciers did a remodeling job on the land. They carved out the valleys of what would become the Colorado, Missouri, and Mississippi Rivers. When the glaciers melted, they left their mark—big puddles that today are some of the world's largest lakes. The greatest are the five Great Lakes, which create part of the border between Canada and the United States.

Where was the island of Hawaii one million years ago?

It was magma, or hot partly melted rock, under Earth's surface. That's because the Hawaiian islands are actually the top of undersea volcanoes.

To remember the names of Great Lakes Huron, Ontario, Michigan, Erie, and Superior, just remember the word "HOMES." Or remember them in order of size, from largest to smallest, with "SHMEO."

According to Hawaiian myth, the Hawaiian fire goddess, Pele, lives in the crater of Mount Kilauea. When the volcano erupts, it's because she's having a temper tantrum.

A volcano is an opening in Earth's surface that forms when lava, gases, and rocks erupt, or burst out, from deep inside Earth. When the rock cools and hardens over time, a mountain forms.

The Pacific islands that make up the state of Hawaii probably formed when volcanoes grew over a hot spot, a place where magma can burst through one of Earth's plates. In the case of the Hawaiian islands, the Pacific plate is moving slowly northwest over such a hot spot, and every once in a while the magma punches through the plate like a heated knife, creating another volcano and another island. On the younger islands, such as the big island of Hawaii, lava continues to flow from the volcanic peaks, creating occasional danger for the residents and beautiful sights for tourists.

What do maps do to Alaska and Hawaii?

Cut and shrink them. When mapmakers try to show all the fifty states of the United States on one page, they often have to shrink the size of Alaska compared to the other states in order to fit it on the page. In reality, Alaska is the largest state in the United States, twice as big as Texas. And both Alaska and Hawaii have long chains of islands that often get cut off in maps. Alaska's Alaska Peninsula and Aleutian Islands stretch for hundreds of miles toward Russia. Hawaii has eight big islands and more than a hundred small ones scattered across the Pacific. These little Alaskan and Hawaiian islands are often chopped off on U.S. maps.

Was Christopher Columbus the first explorer to discover the Americas?

Nope, not by a long shot. The very first "explorers" of the Americas were the ancestors of the American Indians. They may have walked over from Asia between 13,000 and 20,000 years ago. They could have done this because in those years, Asia and Alaska were connected by a "land bridge" that's now underwater. Earth has warmed up since then, and ice that used to be part of the North and South Poles has melted and raised the level of the oceans. Even today, America and Asia are only 52 miles (84 km) apart near the North Pole.

Although no one is sure exactly when the first humans arrived in the Americas, people definitely lived there by about 11,000 B.C. So Columbus didn't "discover" a New World. (It's pretty hard for someplace to be newly discovered when people have lived there for thousands and thousands of years!) He just bumped into land Europeans didn't know was there. And though Columbus insisted that he'd landed in the Indies—thus his naming of the Indians—other Europeans soon saw that the world was really a good deal bigger than they used to think it was.

Then was Christopher Columbus the first sailor to reach the Americas?

No, he wasn't even that. The Viking Eric the Red beat him to it by a good 500 years. Before they were Minnesota's football team, the Vikings were master shipbuilders from Scandinavia who raided, traded, and colonized their way through western Europe, Russia, and North America. Though some Vikings did steal treasure and capture slaves, as a whole they really don't deserve their bad rap as brutish, horn-helmeted thugs. (Vikings did wear helmets, but the helmets didn't have horns.) Most Vikings were merely looking for new trading markets and farmlands.

Good old Eric the Red, however, wasn't doing any of those things. He set sail from Scandinavia because he'd been convicted of manslaughter and was forced to get out of town. So Eric sailed west, happening upon Greenland in the year 983 and starting a small colony there. Around the year 1000, his son Leif Ericsson (get it—son of Eric?) sailed even farther west to what is now Canada. Leif and his men spent the winter and returned to Greenland.

So why do we hear more about Columbus than we do about the Vikings? Because the Vikings didn't stick around the way the Europeans did. After a few years, the Vikings packed up and went home. Their long visit had no lasting impact on North America or Europe.

How green is Greenland?

Not very. Eighty percent of the world's largest island is covered with a thick blanket of ice. But Eric the Red, who named the island, knew that few settlers would come to a colony named "Grayland." So Greenland— and perhaps the world's biggest practical joke—were born.

Why do we celebrate Columbus Day?

To get a day off from school, of course! But really, if Columbus didn't discover America, what did he do?

Columbus started an important migration, or movement of people from one place to another. He brought together people who'd been separated for at least 10,000 years. In what's been called the Columbian exchange, people from across the globe shared ideas, foods, crops, animals, languages, cultures, and religions. Without this exchange, the Americas would have no horses, sheep, pigs, wheat, sugar, and citrus fruit. Europe would be without potatoes, pineapples, peanuts, chocolate and vanilla, corn, turkeys, tomatoes, rubber, and tobacco. Unfortunately for the Americans, Europeans also brought germs. Within 150 years of European arrival, up to 90 percent of the Native American population had died of diseases to which they had no immunity. Most of those who did survive lost their land and traditional ways of life.

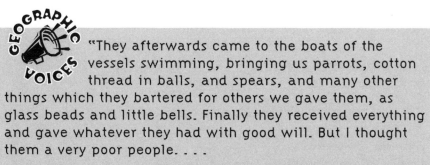

"They afterwards came to the boats of the vessels swimming, bringing us parrots, cotton thread in balls, and spears, and many other things which they bartered for others we gave them, as glass beads and little bells. Finally they received everything and gave whatever they had with good will. But I thought them a very poor people. . . .

"If it please our Lord, I will take six of them from here to our Highness on my departure, that they may learn to speak. The people are totally unacquainted with arms, as our Highness will see by observing the seven I have caused to be taken in. With fifty men all can be kept in subjection, and made to do whatever you desire."

—Christopher Columbus, writing in his diary about the Native Americans he met

Why isn't America called Columbia?

It's all because of one mapmaker. In 1507, mapmaker Martin Waldseemüller named the South American continent after Italian navigator Amerigo Vespucci, who'd sailed to the New World in 1499 and 1501. Unlike Columbus, Vespucci knew that he had reached a New World that wasn't Asia at all. Many Europeans read Vespucci's letters, making his travels more famous in his day than Columbus's. Even though Waldseemüller later took the name "America" off the map, it was too late. The name had stuck, and became attached to the North American continent as well.

If North America had been more like Africa, its history might be very different. Unlike Africa, North America is boat friendly inside and out. Its long coastline and many harbors, rivers, and lakes made it easy for people to travel and explore the continent.

Were people who came to settle in North America immigrants or emigrants?

Both. (Trick question!) An immigrant is someone who comes to a new country. An emigrant is someone who leaves a country to settle in another. So since you have to come to a country from somewhere, to be an immigrant you have to also be an emigrant.

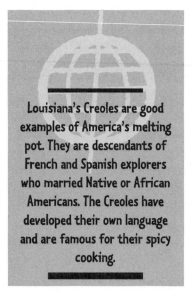

Louisiana's Creoles are good examples of America's melting pot. They are descendants of French and Spanish explorers who married Native or African Americans. The Creoles have developed their own language and are famous for their spicy cooking.

North America is largely a continent of immigrants. By the 1600s, the English, French, and Spanish had started dividing America up into colonies. Many settlers, first from Europe and then from around the world, came seeking adventure, the freedom of the wide open spaces, or the opportunity to make a better life for themselves. Others, like most from Africa, came against their will. Over the years, the United States especially has become known as a "melting pot." Its immigrants—who were emigrants from England, Germany, Italy, Ireland, Russia, Africa, Mexico, Southeast Asia, Central

America, and many more parts of the world—have created a unique mix of cultures, languages, religions, and customs.

Louisiana's Cajuns are a group that hasn't mixed in. These are descendants of French settlers who were forced out of the Acadia region of Canada by the British in the 1750s. They have maintained a separate culture from other Louisiana natives.

What kind of pass did American pioneers need?

Not a hall pass or a bathroom pass, or even a backstage pass for the hottest pioneer bands. They needed a mountain pass, a break or gap in a range of mountains. By the 1740s, settlers in the American colonies were running out of land. They had moved as far west into the continent as they could, but they'd come up against the Appalachian Mountains. The mountains were too rugged to cross, especially with wagons and belongings. There seemed no way through until 1785, when Daniel Boone opened the Wilderness Road through the mountains' Cumberland Gap, near where the states of Virginia, Kentucky, and Tennessee meet. With that frontier open, settlers would keep pushing farther and farther west—across the Mississippi River, the Great Plains, the Rocky Mountains, and other natural obstacles—until they reached the Pacific Ocean along the Oregon, California, and Santa Fe Trails in the 1840s.

"We now had nothing to eat but the raw hides on our roof, which we saved when we butchered our cattle. We had to choose between starving or having snow in the cabin. We chose to eat. Our hides, when boiled in water, softened a little, and the water turned into a thick liquid that resembled glue. It was a most unappetizing mixture."

—Virginia Reed, writing about a trip she made to California when she was only twelve years old. Traveling along the California Trail in 1884, a group of settlers later known as the Donner Party was stranded by an early winter snowstorm. The pass they planned to take through the Sierra Nevada range became sealed with snow. Starving, the party chewed on animal bones and hides, twigs, and even their shoes. Finally, as people died, the survivors ate the bodies of their dead comrades to stay alive. A few people climbed the mountain to find help. When rescuers arrived, only forty-five of the original eighty-nine were alive.

POP QUIZ

Fill in the blank: California is home to the _____ living things on Earth.

a. biggest

b. tallest

c. most glamorous

d. all of the above

The answer is "d." (Well, letter "c" is a matter of opinion, but California is the moviemaking capital of the world.) The tallest living things on Earth are trees. The oldest tree is the bristlecone pine. Some bristlecones have been around for more than 4,000 years. That makes them as old as the pyramids in Egypt. The tallest living things are California redwoods. They aren't as big around as sequoias, but they're taller—often more than 300 feet (91 m) high. That's as high as a football field is long! The Mendocino Tree in northern California is the tallest of the tall at 367 feet 6 inches (112 m) high.

Where is the longest undefended border in the world?

Right between the United States and Canada. This boundary runs for more than 5,000 miles (8,000 km) with only an occasional checkpoint at major roads. The rest is unfenced and unguarded. The fact that no one watches this border is a tribute to the close and generally friendly relations between Canada and the United States. The two countries particularly rely on each other in trade. About 20 percent of U.S. exports go to Canada, with the same amount crossing the line from Canada to the United States. About the same number of tourists cross the border from each country as well.

I'm smelly, dirty, and the United States makes more of me than does any other country. What am I? Garbage. The United States has only 5 percent of the world's population, yet it makes more trash than any other country—more than 200 million tons of garbage each year (about 1,500 pounds per person). It also uses a whopping 45 percent of the world's power.

GEOGRAPHIC VOICES

"Living next to you is in some ways like sleeping with an elephant: No matter how friendly and even-tempered the beast, one is affected by every twitch and grunt."

—Former Canadian Prime Minister Pierre Trudeau, on relations between the United States and Canada

Where in Canada will you feel like you're in France?

In the province of Quebec. Of Canada's ten provinces (which are political divisions like American states), Quebec is least like the others. That's because it was first settled by the French, while much of the rest of Canada was settled by the British. The French lost their Canadian territories to the British in 1763, but the descendants of the French settlers remained.

Helping people of French and English descent live together happily has been one of Canada's biggest challenges. Today there are small groups of French speakers in almost every province, and both French and English are official national languages. But in Quebec, more than 80 percent of the people speak French, and French is the only official language. Some Quebec residents want to become an independent country to preserve their French culture. This may happen in the future. In a 1995 vote, the people rejected the separation by just 51.6 percent to 49.4 percent.

If you vacation in the Caribbean, are you still in North America?

You sure are. Though few people realize it, the vacation lands that are Jamaica, the Virgin Islands, Puerto Rico, and other Caribbean islands are considered part of North America. The islands, which curve from the Gulf of Mexico down toward South America, are actually where Christopher Columbus made his first landfall in the Americas. (And though he did touch on South and Central America, he never laid eyes on mainland North America.)

After Columbus arrived, the Spanish, French, Dutch, English, and other Europeans began settling the Caribbean. The Spaniards tried to enslave the natives and killed many of them in the process. So the Europeans brought slaves from West Africa to work their plantations. When slavery was abolished in the nineteenth century, workers were encouraged to come from China and India. Adding to the islands' unique blend of cultures are immigrants from Lebanon, Syria, Portugal, and other places, who have arrived in more recent years.

Because of their history as European colonies, most Caribbean countries are relatively poor. One of the Caribbean's most important industries is tourism. Vacationers flock to the warmth and beauty of the islands, providing jobs and encouraging the preservation of the fragile environment, which includes precious rain forests.

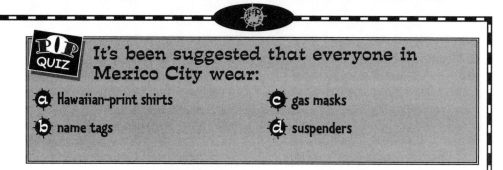

Sadly, the answer is letter "c." Hawaiian shirts would be much more fun, but gas masks are what the inhabitants of Mexico's capital could really use. Mexico City, one of the largest cities in the world, is covered with a brown cloud of car and factory pollution that is extremely unhealthy to breathe.

And that's not the only reason Mexico City is an urban nightmare. Its population of 18 million is growing, and already it's impossible to find houses, jobs, transportation, and food for everyone. Water must be brought in from hundreds of miles away and waste and sewage hauled out. All these problems are made worse by the fact that this part of Mexico is one of the world's worst places to build a city. It has very little fresh water. Even worse, the city is built on a filled-in lake—not very solid ground for a place so close to the Ring of Fire and likely to be hit with violent earthquakes.

Who chose to build Mexico City in such a bad place?

The Aztecs, a wealthy, advanced, and religious people who flourished in Mexico from the fourteenth through the sixteenth centuries. Legend says the Aztecs chose the site for their capital based on a message from one of their gods: Build the seat of your empire where you find an eagle perched atop a cactus, eating a snake. In 1325, they found the spot—a lake in central Mexico. The Aztecs built the enormous city of Tenochtitlán ("place of the cactus") on an island in the lake, with canals and bridges connecting it to the surrounding land. Great pyramids rose in the sacred center of the city, the site of religious sacrifices. Many of those sacrifices, sometimes thousands a year, were human. Aztecs warriors often raided nearby tribes to replenish their supply of offerings to the gods.

Amazingly, the Aztec pyramids and great city were built without the help of animals, metal tools, or the wheel. How? We'll never know. In 1521, the city was captured and nearly destroyed by the Spanish conquistador (conqueror) Hernán Cortés. In their battles against the Aztecs and other native peoples, the Spaniards' horses and guns were almost unnecessary. The smallpox virus they'd unknowingly brought with them was even more deadly. The disease killed 90 percent of the native population. With them died their knowledge, traditions, and city. The Spaniards built their own capital, Mexico City, on top of Tenochtitlán.

CHAPTER 8

SOUTH AMERICA

WHY IS CHILE SHAPED LIKE A CHILI?

BIGGEST, HIGHEST, DEEPEST . . .

Size

Fourth-largest continent: 6,880,454 sq mi (17,819,000 sq km)

Highest mountain

Aconcagua: 22,834 ft (6,960 m)

Lowest point

Valdés Peninsula: 131 ft (40 m) below sea level

Largest lake

Titicaca: 3,200 sq mi (8,287 sq km)

Highest waterfall

Angel Falls: 3,212 ft (979 m)

Are North and South America separate continents?

Like Europe and Asia, North and South America are technically one landmass, connected by the isthmus of Central America. An isthmus is a narrow strip of land that joins two larger landmasses. But as with Europe and Asia, the history of the Americas leads us to think of them separately. When Europeans came to the Americas, Canada and the United States were mostly controlled by the British, while Spain controlled almost everything south of Mexico, including eleven of South America's twelve countries. The twelfth, Brazil, was colonized by Portugal.

Where is South America?

East of North America! Actually, it is south of North America, too, but almost all of South America lies east of Florida.

Do people speak Latin in Latin America?

Only a few who learn it in school. Latin America is often used as another name for Central and South America. It means that most of the people who settled those areas speak languages, such as Spanish and Portuguese, that come from Latin—the language of ancient Rome. However, the people of South America, like those of North America, include many Native Americans, Africans, and settlers from various European countries, so "Latin America" is really a misleading name.

Were Europeans glad to have found the Americas?

Not at first. They just wanted to get to Asia. Once people realized that Columbus hadn't in fact landed in Asia, North and South America quickly became the world's largest roadblock. Sailors searched for a waterway to the Pacific and found it in 1520, when Portugal's Ferdinand Magellan sailed through a twisted sea passage (now called the Strait of Magellan) at the southern tip of South America and continued on into the Pacific. Magellan was killed on the voyage, but his crew continued the journey and sailed all the way back to Spain. Although Magellan didn't make the whole trip, he's usually considered to be the first person to voyage around the world. (The first explorer to actually do this himself was English admiral Sir Francis Drake, in 1580.)

Why is the Land of Fire so cold?

The Land of Fire, or *Tierra del Fuego*, is a collection of freezing, wet, windy islands at the bottom tip of South America. It's called the Land of Fire because the explorer Magellan saw so many campfires built by Native Americans along its shores as he sailed by. This chilly region is far from fiery. In fact, it is only about 700 miles (1,127 km) from Antarctica.

Why do so many South Americans live on the coast?

The interior of South America is full of tropical rain forests and high mountains that aren't easy to live in or farm. So most of its people live along the coast, accessible to the outside world. A few live on the pampas, the flat grasslands where cows graze and gauchos, or South American cowboys, work. (Gauchos, like North American cowboys, have a tradition of being independent. They used to ride their horses barefoot and grip the stirrups with their toes!)

South America is full of natural resources—gold, emeralds, coal, oil, sugar, coffee, and cacao. Still, many of the continent's inhabitants are poor because in many countries most of the land and resources are owned by just a few people.

Is the Amazon a river or an ocean?

It's a river, but in some places it looks like an ocean—at its mouth it is 200 miles (320 km) across. This is wide enough to contain Marajó Island, which is almost as big as Denmark. The mighty Amazon is the largest river in the world. It carries more water than the Nile, Mississippi, and Chang Jian (Yangtze) Rivers put together. The Amazon flows nearly all the way across northern South America, from the mountains of Peru through the rain forests of Brazil. Though the Amazon isn't as long as the Nile, its path is still longer than the highway route from San Francisco to New York City.

POP QUIZ
The Amazon River gets its name from a group of legendary Greek:

a warriors

b Internet companies

c river boats

d water gods

The answer is "a." The Amazon River is named after the Amazon warrior women of Greek mythology. Legends said that these fierce women, who fought in the Trojan war, lived in their own country, doing without men except for a festival once a year. Female children were kept; males ones were swiftly done away with.

So what do these mythical Greek women have to do with South America? The first European to explore the Amazon River, Spain's Francisco de Orellana, claimed that he and his men were attacked by very tall, robust women warriors with bows and arrows. Who could they be but Amazons? he thought. Though no other expeditions reported seeing the female fighters, Orellana's name, River of the Amazons, stuck.

What part of South America could be called the world's biggest steambath?

The half that's covered by the Amazon rain forest, the largest tropical rain forest in the world. With rain falling almost every afternoon, the forest's climate is warm and wet all year round. All that rain makes the forest an explosion of green. Moss carpets the ground and trees, and lush vines creep around the trunks of trees, which are often more than 100 feet (30 m) tall. The plant growth is so dense that it's hard to see all the kinds of animals that live there. The best place to find them is the forest's canopy, the umbrella formed by the treetops.

Tropical rain forests, which lie like a belt around the equator, are home to more kinds of plants and animals than any other place on Earth. Sadly, that rain forest belt is getting smaller every day as loggers cut trees to sell as timber or to create farm and ranchland.

All this destruction is bad for the forests, of course, but it's also bad for all of us. That's because these forests supply a huge amount of the oxygen we need to breathe. Plants of the tropical rain forest are also used to make 25 to 40 percent of our medicines. So many plants are being destroyed before scientists can even discover them that we may have killed all kinds of wonder drugs without ever knowing it.

How is a tropical rain forest like a baseball team?

World of WORDS

The country of Ecuador is named for the equator, which passes through it. South America is more tropical than any other continent because more of it lies near the equator.

Just as everyone on a baseball team works together to win the game, all the living and nonliving things in the rain forest work together. This cooperation is called an ecosystem. The forest's ecosystem includes plants, insects, birds, other animals, soil, climate, and water. The many different species in tropical rain forests make up one of the world's most complex ecosystems.

Every player on a team and every species in the forest is a link in a chain. If one player misses or plays badly in a game, or if one species dies out, everyone else is affected.

Who lives in the Andes Mountains?

Only people named Andy live in the Andes. Just kidding! Not many people at all live in the Andes Mountains, the world's longest and second tallest mountain chain. It's awfully hard to get around in these young, jagged mountains, and the peaks are so tall that most are too cold for farming. Not to mention the fact that many of the mountains are still active volcanoes. The few people who do live in the Andes raise animals such as sheep and llamas, which are sure footed and won't go stumbling down the mountain.

You can find snow just 30 miles (48 km) from the sun-drenched equator atop the steamy volcanic peak of Mount Cotopaxi, in Ecuador. Even near the equator, places of higher elevation are cooler. Also near the equator in the Andes is the snow-covered peak of Mount Chimborazo, where it's so cold you could freeze to death.

Why is Chile shaped like a chili?

Chile stretches like a long and narrow chili pepper down the western coast of South America. That's because the Andes Mountains run along the eastern side of the country, creating a natural border. (But the pepper isn't where Chile got its name. "Chile" comes from a word meaning "where the land ends.") In fact, the Andes run the entire length of South America, from the Caribbean Sea in the north to Cape Horn in the south. That's more than 5,000 miles (8,000 km), long enough that if they were laid across the United States, the mountains would run from the West Coast to the East Coast and far out into the Atlantic! That's why no country in South America spans the width of the continent.

Long and narrow isn't an easy shape for a country to be. Countries that are odd shaped or spread out are harder to keep organized, connected, and defended against invaders. So if you're planning on becoming leader of a country, choose one that's compact and roundish in shape.

How did the Incas get around in the Andes?

They used mountain grasses to weave sturdy rope suspension bridges over rivers and valleys. The Incas were a great civilization of master architects and farmers that flourished in the high plains of the Andes from about the thirteenth century. The Incas built many structures and temples with enormous stones that were fitted together perfectly, without mortar. They created terraced farms in the mountainous land to keep the soil and crops from sliding down the mountain. One of the Incas' greatest accomplishments was Machu Picchu, a sacred walled city nestled high between two peaks where the Andes drop steeply on all sides. Machu Picchu was built on several levels with steep stairways leading to shrines and temples. When the Spanish conquistadors arrived and destroyed the Inca civilization in the 1530s, the city of Machu Picchu went undiscovered because of its distant location. It remained that way until an American found it in 1911. The city appeared to have been abandoned before the Spaniards arrived, but no one knows why.

Chile's Atacama Desert is the driest place on the planet. In some parts, no rainfall has ever been recorded. Like the Himalayas, the Andes act as a barrier to rainfall.

Was there an El Dorado?

The Spanish conquistadors sure hoped so. Soon after Columbus landed in the Americas, the Spanish began conquering their way through South America in search of riches. El Dorado's kingdom was supposed to be the biggest jackpot of all. According to legend, El Dorado was the Golden Man, ruler of a land of gold, whose wealth was far greater than that of any other king in the world.

The story of such a kingdom probably came from the custom of one South American tribe that honored each new chief by covering him with gold dust. The chief washed off the gold in a sacred lake while his people threw in emeralds and more gold. Though the custom ended long before the Spanish arrived, the fantastic story lived on.

The Spanish never found the fabled kingdom, but the idea that it might be around the next bend gave them a reason to keep exploring and taking the natives' land.

POP QUIZ

Which country threw off Spanish rule and became independent in the early nineteenth century?

a Venezuela   **e** Bolivia   **i** Uruguay

b Colombia   **f** Chile   **j** all of the above

c Ecuador   **g** Paraguay

d Peru   **h** Argentina

Okay, it's "j," all of the above. After 300 years as Spanish colonies, all of these countries were tired of having their wealth taken overseas. Between 1810 and 1840, they became independent. Brazil broke away from Portugal a little later, in 1889. Although they rule themselves now, the former colonies still keep the languages and many of the customs of their onetime rulers.

"Moved by your misfortunes, we have been unable to observe with indifference the afflictions you were forced to experience by the barbarous Spaniards, who have ravished you, plundered you, and brought you death and destruction. They have violated the sacred rights of nations. They have broken the most solemn agreements and treaties. In fact, they have committed every manner of crime, reducing the Republic of Venezuela to the most frightful desolation. Justice therefore demands vengeance, and necessity compels us to exact it. Let the monsters who infest Colombian soil, who have drenched it in blood, be cast out forever. . . ."

—Simón Bolívar, in a proclamation to the people of Venezuela in 1813. Bolívar led wars of independence in many of the countries of South America. The country of Bolivia is named after him.

What's the best way to see the world's tallest waterfall?

From the air. Venezuela's spectacular Angel Falls are snuggled so far back among thick tropical forest that they're almost impossible to see unless you're a bird or a pilot. (In fact, the falls weren't discovered by outsiders until 1935, when American pilot Jimmy Angel just happened to fly over them.) The falls drop three times for a stunning total of 3,212 feet (979 m). That's nearly eleven football fields of falls!

How do you shorten the distance around the world by 8,000 miles?

You cut right between North and South America instead of going around both of them. But this wasn't always possible, since there isn't a natural waterway between the continents. People trying to ship goods around the world got tired of going all the way around South America, especially since the waters around Cape Horn are stormy and dangerous. What to do? Build a canal.

In 1904, the United States paid to have a canal, or artificial waterway, built through the isthmus of Panama. Panama is only 31 miles (50 km) wide at its narrowest point, but that's still a lot of canal to dig in the tropical heat and swarms of mosquitoes. For many sailors it was worth it, though. After eleven years of shoveling, a trip from the Atlantic to the Pacific that once took four months now took only about forty-seven days.

Is Rio de Janeiro a river or a month?

Both and neither: it's a Brazilian city named River of January. According to some historians, the Portuguese explorers who landed in Rio's beautiful harbor in the early 1500s arrived on January 1 and thought the harbor was the mouth of a river—hence the name they gave it. In fact, Rio de Janeiro does not lie on any major river, but it is an important port and now one of the world's largest cities.

How are cities like magnets?

Like magnets, cities have a strong force of attraction. Throughout the last third of the twentieth century, cities pulled people off farms in increasing numbers around the world. In cities, these country people are hoping to find better jobs and education. South America is a dramatic example of this. South Americans from the countryside have flocked to such cities as Buenos Aires, Argentina (area population 11,298,000); São Paulo, Brazil (10,018,000); and Lima, Peru (6,321,000). Often these new city dwellers have traded poverty in the country for poverty in the city. On the outskirts of many big South American cities are poor shantytowns, rough huts housing thousands of people who have yet to find a better life.

CHAPTER 9

AUSTRALIA AND NEW ZEALAND

ARE THERE DEVILS IN TASMANIA?

BIGGEST, HIGHEST, DEEPEST . . .

Size

Smallest continent: 2,966,368 sq mi (7,682,300 sq km)

Highest mountain

Kosciuszko: 7,310 ft (2,228 m)

Lowest point

Lake Eyre: 53 ft (16 m) below sea level

Largest lake

Eyre: 3,430 sq mi (8,884 sq km)

Largest island

Tasmania: 26,383 sq mi (68,332 sq km)

POP QUIZ Australia is a:

- **a** continent
- **b** country
- **c** island
- **d** all of the above

The answer is "d." Australia is the only continent that's made up of just one country. (Compare that to Africa's fifty-three!) And that's only one part of what makes the smallest continent special.

Australia is the lowest, flattest, and most sparsely populated nonpolar continent. It is sometimes known as Down Under. That doesn't mean that all the people live underground; it just means that it is entirely south of the equator. But perhaps what makes Australia most interesting is the amazing array of plants and animals found nowhere else on Earth.

Why is Australia home to such unusual animals?

Because Australia has been so far away from the world's other landmasses for the past 100 million years. Animals in Australia developed separately from those that live everywhere else. Australia didn't even have cats, rabbits, or foxes until Europeans brought them.

About half of Australia's native animals are marsupials, like the kangaroo. Marsupials carry their young in a pouch until the babies are fully developed. Some of Australia's curious creatures include the emu, a big nonflying bird that looks like an ostrich; the wallaby, a smaller version of the kangaroo; and the wombat, a marsupial that looks like a bear with a thick snout. But the Most Peculiar Animal Award goes to the duck-billed platypus. The furry animal has the flat bill and webbed feet of a duck and the paddlelike tail of a beaver, yet it lays eggs like a turtle and gives milk to its young like a mammal.

Koalas are among Australia's best-known native animals. Often called koala bears, they're not bears, and they're not as cuddly as they look. The irritable marsupials will scratch and bite if provoked.

Are there devils in Tasmania?

No, but there are Tasmanian devils. These fierce, doglike marsupials are known for their loud, whining voices and huge appetites. They live only on the island of Tasmania, which is south of Australia and makes up one of Australia's six states.

How often can you swim in Lake Eyre?

Oh, about once every 10 to 20 years. All the rest of the time, Australia's largest lake is 3,430 square miles (8,884 sq km) of dry, flat, salty land, with a yearly evaporation (drying) rate 30 times its yearly rainfall. Only five times in the last 100 years did enough rain fall to fill the lake. The unusually wet year of 2000 was one such time. Almost

immediately after the lake filled, millions of shrimp swarmed its salty waters, hibernating frogs emerged to mate, wildflowers bloomed, and fish reappeared, feeding an invasion of seabirds.

The Outback is so dry that the contestants in the Henley-on-Todd Regatta run a race by carrying bottomless boats along the dried-out bed of the Todd River!

What's rare about Australia's deserts?

They're sandy! Not many deserts are, but Australia's are full of sand dunes, sand hills, and sand plains (but not many sand castles). The Great Sandy, the Great Victorian, and the Gibson deserts are in the western part of the continent. The famous landmark of Uluru, or Ayer's Rock, is in the scrubby flat land of the central plain. At 1½ miles (2.4 km) wide and more than 1,100 feet (335 m) high, Uluru is the largest single rock in the world. To

Aborigines, Australia's native people, Uluru is a holy site, a reminder of the spirits who created Earth and all living things in Dreamtime, the time of creation. Aborigines have a close, harmonious relationship with the natural world because they believe that the spirits are their ancestors, living inside trees, rocks, rivers, and animals.

Why is Australia like an inside-out lake?

Because it's dry in the middle but not on the edges. The middle of the continent is just dry grasslands and desert. The few people who live in this rugged land, called the Outback, raise cows and sheep on enormous ranches. The ranchers live so far apart that medical care is provided by the Royal Flying Doctor Service via airplane.

Most of Australia's people live in cities on the outskirts of the continent, where the climate is friendlier and the ocean is just a hop, skip, and a jump away. Still, the entire population of Australia is less than the number of babies born in India each year.

World of WORDS

The Outback gets its name because people used to say that someone who'd gone to the middle of the continent had gone "out to the back country," or spent all day "out back."

What continent did Europeans think Australia might be?

Though there's no record of it happening, it's likely that Asians knew about Australia and might have landed there sometime before Europeans.

HERE'S A HINT: Australia's name comes from Ptolemy's notion of *terra australis incognita*—the unknown southern land. When European sailors first came upon Australia in 1606, they thought it might be part of that legendary southern landmass that was supposed to balance out the world. In 1644, Dutch Captain Abel Tasman sailed all the way around Australia, proving that wasn't the case at all. Tasman also lost four of his men in a violent encounter with the warlike Maoris of the islands of New Zealand. That kept Europeans away until 125 years later, when British Captain James Cook was sent on a secret mission to find out, once and for all, if a southern continent existed. When he didn't find it, the name Australis, which means "southern," went to the most southern continent known at the time—Australia.

Was Australia once a great big jail?

It sure was. The first European settlers, who came to Australia beginning in 1788, were British subjects who were supposed to go to prison. Unfortunately, British jails were already overflowing. The Brits didn't have anywhere else to send their criminals after they lost the rebellious American colonies, so they figured, Why not ship them to Australia?

Most of the lawbreakers weren't hard-core criminals: One man had stolen twelve cucumber plants, and an eleven-year-old had taken a length of ribbon. The criminals actually got a pretty good deal going to Australia instead of to jail. (Especially considering where Russian convicts were sent—Siberia!)

The boomerang was an Aboriginal hunting tool.

True! The Aborigines, the only people in Australia until European settlers came, lived by hunting and gathering for food. They developed the boomerang as a hunting tool thousands of years ago. Aborigines had two types of boomerangs: returning and nonreturning. Returning boomerangs, which were specially curved to come back if the hunter missed his target, were used in traditional sports or to kill small birds. Nonreturning boomerangs were used to kill large game or enemies.

Today, some Aborigines still cling to tribal, or at least semitraditional, ways. Many others work as sheep or cattle farmers in the Outback. But they still have boomerang throwing competitions. The United States, Canada, and Europe compete in the sport as well. There's even a Boomerang World Cup!

GEOGRAPHIC VOICES

"From what I have said of the natives of New Holland they may appear to some to be the most wretched people upon Earth; but in reality they are far happier than we Europeans, being wholly unacquainted not only with the superfluous, but with the necessary conveniences so much sought after in Europe; they are happy in not knowing the use of them."

—James Cook, writing about the Aborigines when he arrived in Australia, which the Dutch had named New Holland, in 1774

If an Australian calls himself a drongo for forgetting to put a shrimp on the barbie, what does he mean? He's using an Aboriginal word to say he's a fool for forgetting to put a shrimp on the barbecue. The Australian version of English has adopted many Aboriginal words and created plenty of its own. Australians especially like to shorten long words and replace the ending with "o." So "arvo" is afternoon, and "garbo" is the garbage collector.

Where were one out of every five Australians born?

Somewhere else. Immigrants have been coming to the continent ever since the first prisoners arrived from England. Britain sent convicts until 1868, and with them came free settlers who wanted to escape crowded Europe and make better lives for themselves. This was especially true after gold was found near Melbourne in 1851.

Most of Australia's immigrants are British, but a good number are from other parts of Europe and from Asia. Many have come looking for jobs and a better life for their families. Some of Australia's most recent immigrants came from Vietnam and Yugoslavia as refugees, or are people who have left their own countries to escape danger and persecution.

Who were Australia's unruliest immigrants?

Not the convicts, but the rabbits brought by Europeans. Australia's first rabbits, twenty-four of them, arrived in 1859. Within fifty years the cute little bunnies had gotten out of hand. Without natural predators, they multiplied like crazy and spread all over the continent, crowding and eating the food of the native animals. At one point the country had about 500 million rabbits, or 50 times its human population. The rabbits munched all the vegetation off the land, starving livestock and turning grasslands into desert. In the twentieth century, Australians deliberately introduced a rabbit-killing disease, which reduced the rabbit population—at least, for a while. Some rabbits may now be resistant to the disease, and the population may rebound.

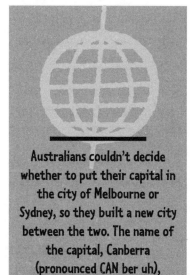

Australians couldn't decide whether to put their capital in the city of Melbourne or Sydney, so they built a new city between the two. The name of the capital, Canberra (pronounced CAN ber uh), means "meeting place."

Australians have learned the hard way that bringing foreign species into an island habitat can be a disaster. Similar problems with nonnative species exist on other Pacific islands, including Hawaii.

Where will you find the world's most beautiful graveyard?

In the warm, shallow water off the northeast coast of Australia. The graveyard is the Great Barrier Reef, the largest group of coral reefs in the world. A coral reef is a rocklike formation that's created by a community of tiny sea creatures called corals. Corals live attached to the reef, building hard outer skeletons to protect their soft bodies. When the corals die, their skeletons become part of the reef. The reef grows little by little by little. The Great Barrier Reef has been growing for thousands of years and is 1,250 miles (2,012 km) long.

The Great Barrier Reef is Australia's biggest tourist attraction. People snorkel in its shallow waters to see the incredible variety of sea life. Among the reef's hundreds of kinds of coral live clams, starfish, sea cucumbers, and about 1,500 different kinds of fish. Many of the fish are brilliantly colored to blend in with the colorful corals.

In what country do most of the inhabitants wear sheepish grins?

In New Zealand, where most of the inhabitants are sheep. The country is one of the world leaders in exporting wool, with fifteen woolly sheep for every person. Most of New Zealand's sheep, and most of its people, live on the country's north island, since its south island is more mountainous.

What did New Zealand give women before any other country in the world?

Not wool sweaters, but the right to vote. New Zealand did this in 1893. Finland followed in 1906, Great Britain in 1918, and the United States in 1920.

What do New Zealand and Iceland have in common?

Viking ancestors? No, hot springs. Like Iceland, the north island of New Zealand is volcanic, with many hot springs and geysers.

POP QUIZ — If you were a kiwi, which of the following would you be?

a) a bird
b) a fruit
c) a New Zealander
d) all of the above

The answer is letter "d." A kiwi is an unusual nonflying bird native to New Zealand; it's also a fruit that grows well in New Zealand. Over time, the people of New Zealand themselves have acquired this nickname.

Which best describes the waters around Australia and New Zealand?

a polka dotted

b striped

c plaid

d paisley

The answer is "a." The South Pacific Ocean near Australia and New Zealand is dotted with more than 25,000 islands, together creating a vast region called Oceania. Most of the islands are small volcanic spots that have erupted from the ocean floor. The islands are usually divided into areas called Micronesia, Melanesia, and Polynesia. Some are territories controlled by France, the United States, and other countries, but among them are twelve independent countries.

Micronesia, Greek for "small islands," is a collection of hundreds of islands, most of which are tiny coral atolls (a circle of coral with a lagoon in the middle). Micronesia has only about 3,000 square miles (7,770 sq km) of land and about 130,000 people.

Melanesia, Greek for "black islands" because of the dark skin of many of its peoples, is dominated by the large island of New Guinea. This area has 80 percent of the region's population and 93 percent of its land.

Polynesia, Greek for "many islands," has many thousands of coral and volcanic islands that are home to 2 million people. The ancient Polynesians were among the first seafarers. They sailed great distances but didn't mark or document their discoveries, so we'll never know exactly what they found or learned.

The island of New Guinea is divided into two political units: Irian Jaya, controlled by Indonesia, and Papua New Guinea, which is an independent country. The diverse peoples of Papua New Guinea speak more languages— over 700—than those of any other country.

CHAPTER 10

ANTARCTICA

IS THERE REALLY A POLE AT THE SOUTH POLE?

BIGGEST, HIGHEST, DEEPEST . . .

Size

Fifth-largest continent:
5,100,400 sq mi
(13,209,000 sq km)

Highest mountain

Vinson Massif: 16,067 ft
(4,897 m)

Lowest point

Bentley Subglacial Trench:
8,327 ft (2,538 m) below sea
level, covered by ice sheet

Coldest spot

Vostok Station: -128.6 °F (-89 °C)
on July 21, 1983

What is the population of Antarctica?

Zero. Antarctica has no
cities and no permanent
residents. Even
penguins spend most of
the year in warmer
places. And no
wonder—the World's
Largest Freezer is the
coldest, windiest, and
driest continent on the
planet. Seals, whales,
and gulls come to feed
in the fish-filled waters
around the coast.
Mosses, lichens, and a
few kinds of insects
survive in Antarctica. Scientists from around the world live there for
months at a time—but not year-round—to do research on Antarctica's
geology, animals, and resources.

How long has Antarctica been on the map?

For sixteen centuries before it was discovered. In the second century A.D., the great Greek geographer Ptolemy wrote a book about the known places of the world (Europe, Asia, and the northern part of Africa). In it, he described a *terra australis incognita*, or "unknown southern land." Like other early philosophers and geographers, Ptolemy believed that there must be a significant landmass in the Southern Hemisphere to balance out the known land in the Northern Hemisphere. Without it, he reasoned, wouldn't the planet be off balance and topple wildly to one side?

That question wasn't answered until the eighteenth century, when English Captain James Cook was sent on a secret mission to put the issue to rest once and for all. Cook made three voyages between 1768 and 1779. Two of them came close to Antarctica, but not close enough to see land. His voyages suggested there was no southern continent after all. Islands off the coast of Antarctica were sighted in 1820 by American whaling captain Nathaniel Palmer. Russia's Admiral von Bellingshausen finally found the mainland in 1820.

Why was Antarctica so hard to find?

Because it's cooooold down there! In the summer, mountains of ice break off from the continent and sometimes clog up the ocean like too many ice cubes in a big punch bowl. Sailing the stormy, foggy seas around Antarctica is like playing Dodge-the-Iceberg. Not only are all those icebergs dangerous, they get in the way of ships coming close to the mainland. Though the ice freezes back together in the wintertime, it's also much colder, and dark, then.

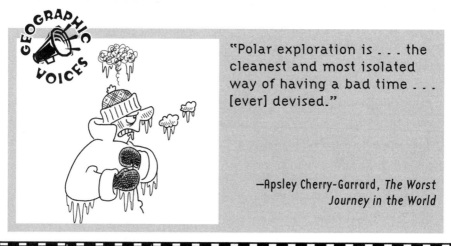

GEOGRAPHIC VOICES

"Polar exploration is . . . the cleanest and most isolated way of having a bad time . . . [ever] devised."

—Apsley Cherry-Garrard, *The Worst Journey in the World*

What happens to your spit in the Antarctic winter?

It freezes before it hits the ground. The lowest temperature on Earth, -128.6 °F (-89 °C), was recorded in Antarctica in 1983. Winter temperatures can be as cold as -125 °F (-87 °C). But in the summer, it can warm up to a relatively warm 0 °F (-18 °C). Antarctica is much colder than the Arctic, in the North. That's because Antarctica has an average elevation of about 6,500 feet (1,980 m), while the Arctic stays at sea level.

"Antarctic" means "the opposite of the Arctic," which is the area around the northern pole of the world. What else is different about the two places?

- The Arctic is an ocean; the Antarctic is land.
- The Arctic is lower and warmer (relatively speaking) than the Antarctic.
- The Antarctic has penguins; the Arctic has polar bears. Neither has trees, and both have seals.

If Antarctica is so dry, where did all its snow and ice come from?

Antarctica is a polar desert where the cold, dry air rarely produces clouds. The small amount of snow that does fall sticks around for thousands of years because it never melts. There hasn't been a lot of action to disturb the Antarctic snow for millions of years. Since the ice preserves ancient rocks and organisms, scientists can learn unique things about Earth's history by drilling into the continent's super-old ice. (Unfortunately, snow from recent years shows dirt and pollution from other parts of the globe.)

If you visit Antarctica's coast, you'll want to wear your triple-thick windbreaker. Cold air dropping down over the center of the continent gives Antarctica's middle portion light winds. The winds pick up, however, as they blow down the icy plateau toward the coast, until they can reach hurricane strength at the shoreline. At Commonwealth Bay, the wind can reach 180 miles an hour (300 km per hour), making it one of the windiest spots on Earth.

What is Antarctica's favorite hat?

An ice cap! The cap of ice that covers Antarctica averages from 6,000 to 15,000 feet (1,829 to 4,572 m) in depth. Most of Earth's fresh water is locked up in this massive ice cube. The thickest ice (15,670 feet, or 4,776 m) is more than ten times higher than the Sears Tower in Chicago.

So what's under all that ice?

You'd hardly know it, but beneath Antarctica's ice rink of a surface there are steep mountains, lakes, and even some active volcanoes. About the only land you can see are the tips of the highest mountains and, in the summer, a few miles of partly thawed shoreline. Scientists estimate that the continent's bedrock has sunk down almost 2,000 feet (about 600 m) under the weight of the ice cap.

Where will you find visitors from outer space?

In Antarctica's ice. More than 16,000 pieces of meteorites have been found in the Antarctic ice sheet. Protected by the dry, cold, stable Antarctic climate, they are in excellent condition and have given scientists much valuable information about the formation of the solar system.

Where is the world's largest unseen lake?

Under the ice in Antarctica. In 1996, scientists using radar discovered a huge, liquid lake 2½ miles (4 km) under the ice cap. At 40 miles (64 km) wide and 1,312 feet (400 m) deep, it's around the size of Lake Ontario. It's also very old. Researchers estimate that the water has been under the ice for 500,000 to 1 million years.

No one is yet sure why this body of water, named Lake Vostok, doesn't freeze. It may be warmed by geothermal heat from beneath. Pressure from the heavy ice above it may keep it liquid, or the ice may protect it from freezing temperatures on the surface. Whatever the reason, biologists are grateful. In 1999, they discovered microbes, tiny life forms, living in the ancient waters of Lake Vostok. These microbes may be similar to life that could be found on Europa, one of the moons of Jupiter.

Where are the world's most gigantic icebergs?

You probably guessed Antarctic waters, but you may not have imagined how big the icebergs are. Antarctic bergs can be as big as states because they break off from the huge ice shelves that ring the continent. In early 2000, scientists spotted the biggest berg in recorded history splitting off from Antarctica's Ross Ice Shelf. Above water, the enormous slab of ice is the size of the state of Connecticut. Below water, it may be ten times larger. The big berg will probably hang around in the waters near Antarctica, where other monster icebergs could break off any day.

Why is it hard to sleep at the South Pole in the summer?

Because it never gets dark. In December, the middle of the Antarctic summer, the Sun never sets at all. In the winter, it's the opposite. The Sun never comes up at all in June and might shine only a few hours in May and July. This "permanent daylight" in summer and "permanent night" in winter comes from the tilt of the Earth.

Is there really a pole at the South Pole?

No and yes. The "pole" in South Pole refers to the end of Earth's axis, the imaginary line that runs through Earth's center from top to bottom. Because this axis doesn't really exist as a physical object, its pole doesn't exist as a real pole, either: it's just a geographic location at 90 degrees south latitude. Still, if you visit the station that's located at the South Pole, you'll see that people there have put up a jokey-looking striped barber's pole to mark the spot.

Do compass needles point north in Antarctica?

No, they point south, to the south magnetic pole. Our planet has two magnetic poles, places where Earth's magnetic field is the strongest. The north and south magnetic poles are not in the same places as the north and south geographical poles. Right now, the south magnetic pole is actually in the ocean just off Antarctica's Commonwealth Bay. It won't stay there, though. For some reason, the magnetic poles move around a bit. Scientists still aren't sure why, but it may have to do with electric currents made in Earth's core.

Which Pole did explorers reach first—North or South?

The North, but not by much. American explorers Robert Peary and Matthew Henson reached the North Pole in 1909. Norwegian explorer Roald Amundsen also had been heading that way when he heard of Peary's achievement. So Amundsen turned around and headed south to conquer the other pole. Another explorer, British Captain Robert Scott, was heading for the South Pole at the same time. Both expeditions wanted their country to have the glory of being the first to reach the South Pole. The race was on.

Amundsen set up his base closer to the South Pole than Scott's so he didn't have as far to travel. Perhaps most importantly, he did what Robert Peary had done in his quest to reach the North Pole—he copied the Eskimos. He traveled faster and more warmly on skis and in Eskimo clothing than Scott did. He used dogs, rather than ponies, to pull his sleds. Amundsen beat Scott to the pole by a month, arriving on December 14, 1911. The disappointed Scott party met bad weather on their return trip, and they all died of frostbite and starvation just miles from their next base station.

"Thursday, 29 March, 1912. . . . Every day we have been ready to start for our depot 11 miles away, but outside the door of the tent it remains a scene of whirling drift. I do not think we can hope for better things now. We shall stick it out to the end, but we are getting weaker, of course, and the end cannot be far. It seems a pity, but I do not think I can write more."

—From Robert Scott's diary, found after his death

Who owns Antarctica?

Good question. The answers are no one and seven different countries. Antarctica has no permanent residents and no government to say who owns it, so other countries have claimed pie-slice-shaped pieces of land. Some of the claims make more sense than others. Australia, New Zealand, Argentina, and Chile all make claims that extend from the southern parts of their countries. Norway claims land because Norwegian Roald Amundsen was the first to reach the South Pole. The United Kingdom makes a claim because Robert Scott wasn't far behind him. France makes a claim because, well, that's one of the ones that doesn't make much sense. Eight other countries, including the United States, have research bases on the continent but don't claim any land.

In 1959, twelve nations signed an Antarctic Treaty that said no more claims could be made on the continent and that the land could be used only for peaceful, scientific purposes. (The twelve nations were Argentina, Australia, Belgium, Chile, France, Japan, New Zealand, Norway, South Africa, the Soviet Union, the United Kingdom, and the United States.) More countries have signed since then. In 1991, another agreement said that no minerals could be taken from the continent and sold.

Why is the sky over Antarctica like a doughnut?

Because there's a big (but invisible) hole in the middle of it. The hole is in the ozone layer of our atmosphere, about 10 to 30 miles (16 to 48 km) above Earth's surface. It usually appears in the spring and stays for several months.

Ozone is a special kind of oxygen. Near ground level, it is a poisonous pollutant that becomes smog. But far away from Earth's surface, ozone forms a thin but essential shield against the Sun's harmful ultraviolet rays. Without any ozone at all, we'd all be long gone. Less ozone means more cases of skin cancer, eye damage, and other health problems, as well as damage to crops and other plants.

The hole in the ozone layer probably came from products like refrigerators and aerosol spray cans, which give off chemicals that eat away at the lifesaving shield. Most countries have stopped using these chemicals, but it still may take a hundred years for the atmosphere to return to health.

Where is Spaceship Earth headed?

Spaceship Earth, our only home, is a precious and fragile place. We must do our best to take care of it, even though we don't always know how. As the late geographer, mapmaker, inventor, and engineer R. Buckminster Fuller once said, "[There is] one outstandingly important fact regarding Spaceship Earth, and that is that no instruction book came with it." The instruction book is one we must write. To do that, we learn as we go—by asking geographic questions about where things are and why and how they got there.

Our ancestors began this process when the first cave people scratched maps in the dirt. We continue the task today. The more we learn about Earth, the better prepared we are to meet the challenges of the third millennium and beyond. But no matter how much we learn, there will always be more questions to ask and new places to explore.

COUNTRIES BY CONTINENT

COUNTRIES CHANGE FROM TIME TO TIME, AND NEW COUNTRIES ARE CREATED.

AFRICA

Algeria
Angola
Benin
Botswana
Burkina Faso
Burundi
Cameroon
Cape Verde
Central African
    Republic
Chad
Comoros
Congo
Côte d'Ivoire
Democratic Republic
    of the Congo
Djibouti
Egypt
Equatorial Guinea
Eritrea
Ethiopia
Gabon
Gambia
Ghana
Guinea
Guinea-Bissau
Kenya
Lesotho
Liberia
Libya
Madagascar
Malawi
Mali
Mauritania
Mauritius
Morocco
Mozambique
Namibia
Niger
Nigeria
Rwanda
São Tomé and
    Principe
Senegal
Seychelles
Sierra Leone
Somalia
South Africa
Sudan
Swaziland
Tanzania
Togo
Tunisia
Uganda
Zambia
Zimbabwe

ASIA

Afghanistan
Armenia
Azerbaijan
Bahrain
Bangladesh
Bhutan
Brunei
Cambodia
China
Cyprus
Georgia
India
Indonesia
Iran
Iraq
Israel
Japan
Jordan
Kazakhstan
Kuwait
Kyrgyzstan
Laos
Lebanon
Malaysia
Maldives
Mongolia
Myanmar
Nepal
North Korea
Oman
Pakistan
Philippines
Qatar
Saudi Arabia
Singapore
South Korea
Sri Lanka
Syria
Taiwan*
Tajikistan
Thailand

* Its inhabitants consider
Taiwan an independent
country, but China
considers it a province
of China.

Turkey
Turkmenistan
United Arab
  Emirates
Uzbekistan
Vietnam
Yemen

EUROPE

Albania
Andorra
Austria
Belarus
Belgium
Bosnia and
  Herzegovina
Bulgaria
Croatia
Czech Republic
Denmark
Estonia
Finland
France
Germany
Greece
Hungary
Iceland
Ireland
Italy
Latvia
Liechtenstein
Lithuania
Luxembourg
Macedonia
Malta
Moldova
Monaco
Netherlands
Norway
Poland
Portugal
Romania
Russia

San Marino
Slovakia
Slovenia
Spain
Sweden
Switzerland
Ukraine
United Kingdom
Vatican City
Yugoslavia

NORTH AMERICA

Antigua and
  Barbuda
Bahamas
Barbados
Belize
Canada
Costa Rica
Cuba
Dominica
Dominican Republic
El Salvador
Grenada
Guatemala
Haiti
Honduras
Jamaica
Mexico
Nicaragua
Panama
Saint Kitts and
  Nevis
Saint Lucia
Saint Vincent and
  the Grenadines
Trinidad and Tobago
United States

SOUTH AMERICA

Argentina
Bolivia
Brazil
Chile
Colombia
Ecuador
Guyana
Paraguay
Peru
Suriname
Uruguay
Venezuela

AUSTRALIA, NEW ZEALAND, OCEANIA

Australia
Fiji
Kiribati
Marshall Islands
Micronesia
Nauru
New Zealand
Palau
Papua New Guinea
Samoa
Solomon Islands
Tonga
Tuvalu
Vanuatu

MILESTONES

The letter "c" before a date means "circa," or "about."

B.C.

10,000–8000 The first villages arise in the Middle East.

c. 5000 Sailing ships are used on rivers in Mesopotamia.

2800–1500 Stonehenge is built. This ancient stone circle in England is probably a religious center and astronomical clock.

c. 2300 A map of the city of Lagash is made in Mesopotamia.

c. 2000 Walled settlements arise in northern China.

c. 1800 Pyramid shrines are built in the Andes.

c. 1600 Settlers colonize Pacific islands.

c. 1500 Olmec culture arises in Mexico.

c. 900 Babylonians create the first known world map.

c. 850 Homer dictates the *Odyssey*, the first literary geographic work.

c. 750 Greek city-states begin to expand throughout the Mediterranean.

c. 600 The African city of Meroë becomes a center of ironworking and trade.

c. 530 Pythagoreans in Greece teach that the world is round, not a disk.

c. 320–310 Aristarchus says Earth revolves around the Sun.

c. 240 Eratosthenes calculates distance around Earth.

214 Construction of the Great Wall of China begins.

c. 190–120 Greek astronomer Hipparchus is the first to use latitude and longitude.

c. 112 The Silk Road opens across central Asia, allowing trade between China and Europe.

c. 10 Greek geographer Strabo's seventeen-volume *Geography* describes the world as it was known to people of the Mediterranean.

A.D.

100 The Roman Empire is at its height.

c. 130 In his major works, Ptolemy places "north" at the top of the map and says Earth is the center of the solar system.

271 The magnetic compass is used in China.

618 The Tang dynasty arises in China and takes control of much of the Silk Road. Its capital, Chang'an, has more than one million people.

700 Pueblo villages arise in the American Southwest.

c. 1000 Vikings colonize parts of North America but don't leave a lasting impact in the area.

1095 The Christian Crusades begin, stimulating contact and trade with the East.

1206 Mongols, under Chingis Khan, begin conquering Asia.

1275 Marco Polo arrives in China.

c. 1325 The great African traveler Ibn Battuta begins his journeys through Africa and Asia.

c. 1440 Prince Henry the Navigator of Portugal sends men to explore the coast of Africa.

1444 The Portuguese bring the first African slaves to Europe.

1487 Bartholomeu Dias sails around the southern tip of Africa.

1492 Christopher Columbus arrives in the Caribbean.

1497 Italy's Giovanni Caboto, working for England, reaches Newfoundland, North America.

1497–8 Vasco da Gama is the first European to sail to India and back.

1499 Amerigo Vespucci reaches America.

1505 The Portuguese set up trading centers in East Africa.

1507 The Waldseemüller map names the New World after Amerigo Vespucci.

1513 Spaniard Vasco Núñez de Balboa is the first European to sight the Pacific Ocean.

1519–22 Ferdinand Magellan's ship is the first to sail around the world.

1521 Spaniard Hernán Cortés captures the Aztec capital of Tenochtitlán.

1532 Spain's Francisco Pizarro conquers the Incas in Peru.

1543 Polish astronomer Nicolaus Copernicus says Earth revolves around the Sun.

1577–80 Sir Francis Drake is the first Englishman to sail around the world.

1584 English explorer Sir Walter Raleigh unsuccessfully tries to establish a colony in Virginia.

1588 The English defeat the Spanish Armada, beginning England's rule of the seas.

1606 Dutch sailors sight the coast of Australia.

1607 The first permanent English settlement in North America is founded at Jamestown, Virginia.

1609 The telescope is invented; Galileo uses it to confirm that Earth revolves around the Sun.

1620 English Pilgrims sail to Massachusetts on the *Mayflower*.

1645 Dutch sailor Abel Tasman sails around Australia and discovers New Zealand.

1675 Greenwich Observatory is founded in England and becomes the world's leading scientific center.

1772 English Captain James Cook is sent to look for Antarctica; he doesn't find it, but maps Australia.

1803 In the Louisiana Purchase, American President Thomas Jefferson buys a huge amount of land from France, more than doubling the size of the United States.

1804–6 Lewis and Clark map a route to the Pacific across western North America.

1825 The first practical railroad service begins in London.

1830 World population is one billion.

1831–36 Charles Darwin, a British naturalist, sails the coast of South America and begins to develop his revolutionary theory of natural selection.

1841–73 Scottish missionary David Livingstone explores the interior of Africa.

1848–49 Tens of thousands of settlers throng the American West in the California gold rush.

1854 American Commodore Matthew Perry opens Japan to Westerners after 250 years of Japanese isolation.

1856 Mount Everest is declared the highest mountain in the world.

1869 The "Golden Spike" is hammered in at Promontory Point, Utah, completing the first transcontinental railroad across the United States.

1869 The Suez Canal opens between the Mediterranean and Red Seas, cutting more than 4,000 miles (6,400 km) off the route from England to India.

1872 The United States Geological Survey is founded; it will map the entire United States.

1903 The first successful airplane is launched at Kitty Hawk, North Carolina, by Orville and Wilbur Wright.

1909 American explorer Robert Peary and his assistant Matthew Henson reach the North Pole.

1911 Norwegian explorer Roald Amundsen reaches the South Pole, beating the British Scott expedition by a month.

1913 The line of longitude that runs through the Greenwich Observatory becomes accepted as the prime meridian.

1914 The Panama Canal opens, linking the Atlantic and Pacific Oceans and shortening a trip around the world by nearly 8,000 miles (12,900 km).

1914–18 World War I results in the redrawing of maps of Europe and its colonies.

1917 The Trans-Siberian Railroad, the longest railroad in the world, connects Moscow to the Sea of Japan, opening Siberia to development.

1922 The Union of Soviet Socialist Republics (Soviet Union) is proclaimed.

1925 The first skull of an australopithecine is found in Africa.

1927 American aviator Charles Lindbergh makes the first solo, nonstop flight across the Atlantic in his plane, the *Spirit of Saint Louis*.

1939–45 World War II redraws boundaries in Europe and Asia.

1945 The United Nations is founded.

1948 The state of Israel gains independence.

1953 Sir Edmund Hillary of New Zealand and Tenzing Norgay of Nepal are the first to reach the summit of Mount Everest.

1957 The first space satellite, *Sputnik I,* is launched by the Soviet Union.

1961 Soviet cosmonaut Yuri Gagarin is the first person in space.

1964 The Aswan High Dam on the Nile is completed. Built to irrigate and provide hydroelectric power for Egypt, it profoundly changes the Nile ecosystem.

1969 American Neil Armstrong is the first human to walk on the moon.

1970 The first Earth Day is celebrated to increase awareness of protecting the environment.

1975 World population reaches four billion.

1984 The first hole in the ozone layer is found over Antarctica.

1984 Soviet researchers in Siberia drill the world's deepest hole, reaching Earth's lower crust.

1990 Apartheid ends in South Africa.

1990 The Hubble space telescope is launched, allowing scientists to see almost to the ends of the universe.

1990 The World Wide Web is launched, making the Internet more user-friendly.

1991 The Soviet republics declare their independence, ending the Soviet Union.

1992 The former Yugoslavia breaks into five new republics.

1999 World population reaches six billion.

GLOSSARY

acid rain: rainwater that contains acid-forming chemicals as a result of air pollution

apartheid: South Africa's former system of legal racial discrimination

archipelago: a string or chain of islands

arid: dry and barren; without enough water for things to grow

atlas: a book of maps

atmosphere: the blanket of air that surrounds a planet

atoll: a ring-shaped coral island with a lagoon in the middle

bay: a small body of water partially surrounded by land

bematist: someone who estimates distances by measuring his or her steps

canal: an artificial waterway

canyon: a long narrow valley that rises steeply on both sides

cardinal directions: the main directions on a compass—north, south, east, and west

carrying capacity: the greatest number of people an area can support with its food, water, and other resources

cartographer: a person who makes maps

circumference: the distance around a circle or sphere

climate: weather patterns over time

climate map: a map that shows an area's climate

colony: an area of land controlled by another country

compass rose: a feature on a map that points to north, south, east, and west

continent: one of the major landmasses on Earth

continental divide: a line of high mountains that separates river systems that flow to different sides of a continent

continental drift: the theory that today's continents were once one landmass and have drifted apart over millions of years

coral reef: a colorful formation made of coral skeletons in warm, shallow water

country: the territory of, or land that belongs to, a nation

culture: the ideas, art, knowledge, and tools of a particular people at a certain time

current: a stream of water that flows in a certain direction along or under the surface of a body of water, such as a stream, river, or ocean

cyclone: a large, spinning storm

delta: a triangular, fertile area of land around the mouth of a river

desert: an area of land that receives less than 10 inches (25 cm) of rain a year

desertification: the growth of a desert due to loss of vegetation earthquake: waves in Earth's surface caused by movement along fault lines

East: regions in the Eastern Hemisphere

ecosystem: a group of living things that depend on one another and on the environment in which they live

elevation: the height of an area above sea level

emigrant: someone who moves away from his or her native country

El Niño: a warm ocean current that flows from the eastern Pacific Ocean

equator: the imaginary line around the center of Earth at zero latitude

erosion: the gradual wearing away of rock or soil by wind, water, or ice

famine: long periods of extreme food shortage that affect a large area

fault: a crack in Earth's surface

fjord: a tall, narrow coastal inlet formed by rivers and glaciers

fossil: the remains of a plant or animal that lived long ago

fossil fuel: a fuel such as coal, oil, or natural gas that is made from the remains of plants or animals that lived long ago

glacier: a huge sheet of ice and snow

greenhouse effect: the gradual warming of Earth caused by too much carbon dioxide and other harmful gases in the atmosphere

gulf: a large portion of the ocean, partially surrounded by land

harbor: a sheltered area of a body of water where ships can dock

hemisphere: one half of the world

hurricane: a huge, circling tropical storm that usually brings heavy rains and high winds

ice age: any historic period when ice sheets and glaciers covered much of Earth's surface, the last one ending about 10,000 years ago

immigrant: someone who comes to a new country

international date line: an imaginary line in the Pacific Ocean at about 180 degrees longitude that separates one day from the next

island: a landmass, smaller than a continent, that is completely surrounded by water

isthmus: a narrow strip of land connecting two larger pieces of land

lake: a large body of water surrounded by land

latitude: how far north or south of the equator a place is, measured by imaginary lines that circle Earth horizontally

lava: hot liquid rock that erupts from a volcano

leeward: the side of an object that is away from the wind

legend: the key on a map that explains what the symbols mean

longitude: how far east or west of the prime meridian a place is, measured by imaginary lines that cross Earth from pole to pole

magma: hot, liquid rock beneath Earth's surface

mantle: the part of Earth that lies between the core and the crust

map: a representation of a place or an area of Earth's surface

migration: movement of peoples or animals from one place to another monsoon: a wind that changes direction with the seasons

mountain: a mass of rock high above the surrounding land

nation: a group of people, usually of a common culture, that has or wants to have a single government

nonrenewable resource: a natural resource that cannot be made again once it is used up

ocean: the huge body of salt water that covers nearly three-quarters of Earth; or one of the four main sections of the world ocean: Arctic, Atlantic, Indian, and Pacific

ozone: a special kind of oxygen in Earth's atmosphere that protects life from the Sun's ultraviolet rays

pampas: flat grasslands of South America

pangaea: the supercontinent that existed 220 million years ago

parallel: a line of latitude

peninsula: a long piece of land surrounded on three sides by water

permafrost: permanently frozen soil

physical map: a map that shows the physical features of an area, such as mountains or rivers

plain: a large, flat, and mostly treeless area of land

plate: a large piece of Earth's crust

plateau: an area of high, flat land

political map: a map that shows boundaries, countries, cities, and capitals

pollution: material that contaminates the air, water, or soil

population: the number of living things in a certain area

prime meridian: the line of zero longitude, which runs through Greenwich, England

projection: the process of showing the round Earth on a flat surface, such as a map

rain forest: a forest that receives heavy rainfall and is rich in plant and animal life

refugee: a person who flees his or her own country because of danger there

region: an area of Earth that has at least one common physical or human characteristic

relief map: a map that shows an area's elevation above sea level

renewable resource: a natural resource that can be continuously restored

Richter scale: a system of numbers that measures the energy released by an earthquake

savanna: an area of tropical grasslands

scale: the relationship between the measurement on a map and the actual distance on Earth's surface

sea: a smaller section of an ocean

sea level: the level of the ocean's surface

solar system: all the planets, moons, and bodies that travel around the Sun

steppe: a cool, treeless plain with short grasses

strait: a narrow channel of water that connects two larger bodies of water

state: a group of people united under one government; or the political units that make up a country

taiga: a cold, subarctic evergreen forest

temperate: a climate without extreme heat or cold

Third World: a term once used to describe underdeveloped countries

tide: the twice-daily rise and fall of the ocean

topography: physical features

tornado: a violent storm with a quickly rotating column of air

tropics: the warm area that extends 23 degrees latitude north and south of the equator

tsunami: an enormous, fast-moving ocean wave caused by an earthquake

tundra: a cold, treeless plain with permanently frozen subsoil

typhoon: a hurricane that begins in the western Pacific Ocean

volcano: an opening in Earth's surface that forms when lava, gases, and rocks erupt, or burst out, from deep inside Earth

West: regions in the Western Hemisphere

windward: the side of an object that faces the wind

SELECTED BIBLIOGRAPHY

Bell, Neill. *The Book of Where: Or How to Be Naturally Geographic*. Boston: Little, Brown, 1982.

Davis, Kenneth C. *Don't Know Much About® Geography*. New York: Avon Books, 1992.

Demko, George. *Why in the World: Adventures in Geography*. New York: Anchor Books, 1992.

Farndon, John. *Dictionary of the Earth*. London: Dorling Kindersley, 1994.

Fritz, Jean. *Around the World in a Hundred Years*. New York: Putnam & Grosset Group, 1994.

Glicksman, Jane. *Cool Geography*. New York: Price Sterling Sloan, 1998.

MacDonald, Fiona. *Explorers: Expeditions and Pioneers*. New York: Franklin Watts, 1994.

Marshall, Bruce, ed. *The Real World: Understanding the Modern World Through the New Geography*. London: Houghton Mifflin, 1991.

Mason, Antony. *The Children's Atlas of Exploration*. Brookfield, CT: The Millbrook Press, 1993.

National Geographic Society. *Exploring Your World: The Adventure of Geography*. Washington, DC: National Geographic Society, 1993.

Newby, Eric. *The World Atlas of Exploration*. New York: Rand McNally, 1975.

The Random House Atlas of the Oceans. New York: Random House, 1991.

Rosenthal, Paul. *Where on Earth*. New York: Alfred A. Knopf, 1992.

Sherer, Thomas E., Jr. *The Complete Idiot's Guide to Geography*. New York: Alpha Books, 1997.

Stefoff, Rebecca. *Accidental Explorers*. New York: Oxford University Press, 1992.

————. *Women of the World: Surprises and Side Trips in the History of Discovery*. New York: Oxford University Press, 1992.

Tufty, Barbara. *1001 Questions Answered About Earthquakes, Avalanches, Floods and Other Natural Disasters*. New York: Dover Publications, 1969.

Waechter, John. *Man Before History*. Oxford, England: Phaidon Press, 1976.

Watson, Benjamin A. *The Old Farmer's Almanac Book of Weather & Natural Disasters*. New York: Random House, 1993.

Wonders of the World. Chicago: World Book, 1997.

World Geography. Alexandria, VA: Time Life Books, 1999.

INDEX

Mercator projection, 42
Mesopotamia, 61, 130
meteorologists, 23. *See also* weather
Mexico, 8, 84, 90, 130
Mexico City, 95–96
Micronesia, 118
Middle East, 61, 65–66, 130
Missouri, earthquake in, 10
Missouri-Mississippi River, 49, 83, 86, 91
Mongols, 63, 64, 131
monsoons, 60, 70
moon
  tides and, 19
  walking on, 45, 134
Mount Aconcagua, 16, 97
mountains
  age of, 15
  building of, 22
  highest, 16
  rain caused by, 60
  See also volcanoes
Mount Chimborazo, 102
Mount Cotopaxi, 102
Mount El'brus, 16, 71
Mount Everest, 16, 58, 133
Mount Kilauea, 86
Mount Kosciuszko, 16, 108
Mount McKinley (Denali), 16, 83
Mount Vesuvius, 13, 14

-N-

nations, 37
Native Americans (American Indians), 87, 89, 98, 131
Netherlands, 79–80, 82
New Guinea, 118
New Zealand, 77, 112, 117, 126, 132
Nile River, 22, 46, 48–49, 61, 134
North America, 83–96
Northern Hemisphere, 24, 32, 38, 120
North Pole, 31, 42, 44, 83, 87, 124–25
Norway, 77, 126
nuclear power, 32

-O-

Ob-Irtyish River, 49
Oceania, 118
oceans, 17–21, 45
  currents in, 19, 78
  number of, 17, 20
oil, 66
Orellana, Francisco de, 100
ozone layer, 126–27, 134

-P-

Pacific Ocean, 18, 20, 43, 98, 115, 118, 130–32
pampas, 99
Panama, 84, 106, 133
Pangaea, 8
Paraguay, 104
parallels, 42
Peary, Robert, 124, 133
permafrost, 67
Persian Gulf, 21
Peru, 99, 104, 107, 132
Polo, Marco, 64, 72, 73, 131
Polynesia, 118
population, 33, 57, 58, 83, 119, 132, 134
Portugal, 10, 54, 82, 94, 97, 131
prime meridian, 43, 133
Ptolemy, 36, 38, 112, 120, 131

-Q-

Quebec, 93–94

-R-

rain forests, 27, 30, 94, 99–101
Richter scale, 12
Ring of Fire, 12, 13, 69
Rio de Janeiro, 107
rivers, 22, 49, 99
Rocky Mountains, 91
Roman Catholic Church, 80
Romania, 82
Russia (*former* Soviet Union), 16, 58, 51, 67–68, 81, 87, 90, 126, 133–34